I0881603

THE BERLIN COLD WAR COMPANION 1945-1989

THE BERLIN COLD WAR COMPANION 1945-1989

DAVID McCORMACK

FONTHILL

Fonthill Media Language Policy

Fonthill Media publishes in the international English language market. One language edition is published worldwide. As there are minor differences in spelling and presentation, especially with regard to American English and British English, a policy is necessary to define which form of English to use. The Fonthill Policy is to use the form of English native to the author. David McCormack was born and educated in Bolton, Lancashire; therefore, British English has been adopted in this publication.

Fonthill Media Limited
Stroud House
Russell Street
Stroud GL5 3AN

Fonthill Media LLC
12 Sires Street
Charleston SC 29403

www.fonthillmedia.com
office@fonthillmedia.com

First published in the United Kingdom
and the United States of America 2019

British Library Cataloguing in Publication Data:
A catalogue record for this book is available from the British Library

ISBN 978-1-78155-728-0

Typeset in 10.5pt on 13pt Sabon
Printed and bound in England

This book is dedicated to the memory of my dear friend Phil Murphy with whom I shared many madcap adventures over the years.

Acknowledgements

My heartfelt thanks to Sharon Schollenberger and Jenny Young for their sterling work as my sounding-boards and proof-readers on this project. Also, I must thank my good friends on both sides of the pond for their continued support and encouragement.

CONTENTS

Acknowledgements 6

1 Exploring Cold War Berlin and Potsdam 9
2 Disagreement piled up on the Shelves 13
3 Nuclear Politics 18
4 Potsdam Viewpoints 28
Viewpoint (A1): Cecilienhof Palace 28
Viewpoint (A2): KGB Prison Museum 31
Viewpoint (A3): Glienicke Bridge 33
5 'A Splendid Analysis' 38
6 Sinews of Peace 44
7 Strategic Philanthropy 48
8 Templehof Viewpoints 61
Viewpoint (B1): Hunger Fork Memorial 61
Viewpoint (B2): Templehof Airport 63
9 The First and Last—Wilhelm Pieck 65
10 'We are all of Berlin' 75
11 Better than War 84
12 Jumping Into the Ring—Günter Grass 95
13 Aggression in Felt Slippers 101
14 Mitte-Moabit-Gesundbrunnen-Alexanderplatz-Friedrichshain-Kreuzberg Viewpoints 103
Viewpoint (C1): DDR Mural and 17 June 1953 Memorial 103
Viewpoint (C2): Berlin Wall Section (Niederkirchnerstraße) 105
Viewpoint (C3): Checkpoint Charlie 108

Viewpoint (C4): Haus am Checkpoint Charlie 115
Viewpoint (C5): Günter Litfin Memorial 116
Viewpoint (C6): The Berlin Wall Memorial Ensemble on Bernauer Straße 118
15 Tilting at Socialist Windmills—Erich Mielke 120
16 Lichtenberg-Hohenschönhausen Viewpoints 130
Viewpoint (D1): Stasi Headquarters Museum 130
Viewpoint (D2): Berlin-Hohenschönhausen Memorial 132
17 Radical Consciousness and the New Sensibility—Rudi Dutschke 134
18 Kreuzberg-Mariendorf Viewpoints 146
Viewpoint (E1): Kreuzberg: Axel Springer Haus & Rudi Dutschke Straße 146
Viewpoint (E2): Charlottenburg: Architecture Building (Berlin Institute of Technology) 149
19 A Gangster Drama 152
20 Authority Gives Way to Possibility 176
21 Steglitz-Zehlendorf Viewpoints 186
Viewpoint (F1): The Allied Museum 186
Viewpoint (F2): The Day the Wall Came Down Sculpture 188
22 Coda 189
Select Bibliography 191

1

Exploring Cold War Berlin and Potsdam

The purpose of this Cold War companion is to encourage and assist people in visiting sites in Berlin and Potsdam where the thin veneer of the Grand Alliance dissolved into a whirlpool of distrust and antagonism. There are, of course, various organised tours run by a number of long-established battlefield tour operators, such as Leger Battlefield Tours, and Stephen Ambrose Historical Tours (aimed at American visitors). These tours usually last between seven and twelve days and provide an excellent introduction for those keen to know more about political and military history, or those who are visiting historical sites for the first time. For single travellers, there is the advantage of being part of a group which share similar interests, added to which there is the possibility of socialising in the evenings. Tour operators take the strain off passengers who may be unfamiliar with foreign travel, or those who simply wish to have an 'all inclusive' experience in which transfers, accommodation, and guided excursions are part of an overall package.

While organised tours generally provide good value-for-money, they are not necessarily the best option for the more seasoned traveller who may feel constrained by tight itineraries which leave limited time slots to see individual viewpoints on the Cold War landscape. Also, those with more in-depth knowledge of the subject can sometimes feel a little frustrated by the delivery of the guide/speaker who is obliged to cater for a wide audience. Travelling independently removes many of the time constraints imposed by organised tours, as you essentially become your own tour manager. This of course takes a certain degree of confidence, and plenty of energy and effort. This Companion will make the process of organising and conducting your own tour of Cold War Berlin less stressful and, hopefully, more enjoyable.

Travelling independently can of course raise a few practical issues. Long periods of driving require more than one person to take their turn at the wheel. Furthermore, actually getting to your desired location can also present problems. While 'sat nav' addresses have been provided for every viewpoint, experience shows that it is always wise to back up the device with a good map (or paper sat nav as it is known in the trade)! If you plan to make extensive use of your 'sat nav', it would be a good idea to ensure that you install the latest map updates. In addition to navigational aids, a mobile phone is an essential piece of kit. It is advisable to have the numbers for your hotels, car hire, and local emergency services stored in your phone before you set off on your adventure.

Visiting historical sites is a hugely worthwhile experience in that it brings the history to life. There is simply nothing to compare with being at the site of a particular action, to literally walk in the footsteps of heroes (or in some cases villains)! The author, who has visited Cold War related sites for over thirty years and has worked as a battlefield guide since 2012 can attest to the value in visiting historical sites, either as part of an organised tour, or as an independent traveller. Above all, no matter how you choose to travel, enjoy the experience.

Visiting Cold War Berlin & Potsdam

If you are planning to fly to Berlin and then rent a car, there are currently two operating airports, Tegel and Schönefeld. A third airport Berlin Brandenburg was due to open in the second half of 2017. However, numerous delays have seen the completion date and scheduled opening put back several times. Eleven years of planning and construction failures have resulted in the scandal of this unused airport becoming something of a hot topic amongst Berlin residents. Indeed, a former project planner involved in this long running farce has forecast that the airport may never open to the public. In the meantime, additional investment has been put into the existing airports in order to cope with rising passenger numbers.

Car hire is fairly simple as there are a number of firms to choose from, including Avis, Europcar and Enterprise Rent-A-Car. If you are driving from the UK, there is the option of either taking a ferry or going via Eurotunnel. There are plenty of advantages in using your own transport, but it will significantly increase your driving time. It is also advisable to look at the websites of the AA and RAC as part of your tour preparation, as both provide good advice regarding driving in Europe.

There is a wide variety of accommodation in Berlin to choose from depending upon your tastes and budget. There are plenty of websites such as Trivago and Expedia which will help you in making your accommodation choices. If you are looking towards a quirkier hotel experience, these locations offer something slightly different from the norm:

Hotel Hüttenpalast: HobrechtStraße 66, Neukoln (huettenpalast.de).
Ostel Hotel: Wriezener Karree 5, Friedrichshain (ostel.eu).
Michelberger Hotel: Warschauer Straße 39, Friedrichshain) michelbergerhotel.com).
Nürnberger Eck: Nürnberger Straße 24 A, Charlottenberg (Nuernberger—eck.de).
If you are looking at staying in hostel type accommodation, these locations offer a comfortable stay at a reasonable price:
Baxpax Kreuzberg Hostel: Skalitzer Straße 104, Kreuzberg (baxpax.de/kreeuzberg).
Pfeffersbett: Hof 4, Haus 6, ChristinenStraße 18-19, Prenzlauer Berg (pfefferbett.de).
The Circus Hostel: Weinsbergsweg 1a, Mitte (circus-berlin.de)
Kima Hotel—Pension: WielanStraße 27, Charlottenburg (hotel-kima.de)
An early start (08:00–08:30hrs) is advised on touring days as time is always the enemy, particularly if you feel tempted to visit sites which lure you away from your planned itinerary. This guide is all about making your visit to the battlefields of Berlin easier. It is in no way prescriptive, and you can of course deviate from the suggested tour routes.

Recommended Maps

For Potsdam, the author recommends the 1:20,000 scale *ADAC Stadt Atlas: Berlin/Potsdam*, the 1:70,000 scale Kompass Berlin/Potsdam und Umgebung, and the 1:125,000 scale *Ausflugskarte Berlin, Potsdam und Umgebung unterwegs zwischen Bad Belzig, Brandenburg an der Havel, Oranienburg, Strausberg, Erkner and Markisch Buchholz.*
For the city of Berlin, the author recommends the 1:20,000 scale *Insight Flexi Map: Berlin*, the 1:20,000 scale Michelin Berlin: Street Map (Laminated), and the 1:15,000 scale *Marco Polo: Berlin City Map.* Additional resources include the excellent Past Finder Zik Zak Berlin and the *Past Finder Berlin 1945–1989 Guide Book*. It is always a worthwhile idea to purchase maps before setting off as this will give you time to become more familiar with the ground. All of the maps and guides can be purchased on sites such as Amazon or eBay.

Cycle Routes

Using bicycles to explore historical sites is becoming increasingly popular among both independent travellers and tour companies. There are numerous cycle rental outlets in Berlin and many of the larger hotels also offer a rental service. Cycling in Berlin is not for the faint hearted as a certain amount of the kamikaze spirit is required to get around. Printable PDF maps of Berlin cycle routes can be obtained from www.berlinmap360.com website.

Suggested Reading

Prior to starting your exploration of Cold War Berlin and Potsdam, the author recommends the following titles for background reading and research:

Michael Dobbs—*Six Months in 1945: From World War to Cold War*
John Lewis Gaddis—*The Cold War*
Jeremy Isaacs & Taylor Downing—*Cold War*
Robert Service—*The End of the Cold War 1985–1991*
J. Smith & Andre Moncourt—*The Red Army Faction A Documentary History* volume 1

Suggested Viewing

Bridge of Spies—Tom Hanks
Funeral in Berlin—Michael Caine
The Baader Meinhof Complex—Martina Gedeck
The Rise and Fall of the Berlin Wall—The History Channel
The Spy Who Came in From The Cold—Richard Burton

2

Disagreement piled up on the Shelves

As Stalin prepared for the 'Big Three' conference at Yalta, he could feel satisfied that his image, and that of the Soviet state stood in high esteem throughout the world. The abolition of the Comintern in May 1943 appeared to signal the end of Soviet expansionism. Meanwhile, feats of valour displayed by the Red Army became well known, particularly the heroic defence of Leningrad and Stalingrad. In much of liberated Europe resistance movements were being increasingly associated with their Communist members. Across Europe, significant numbers of the population seriously began to consider whether Communism offered a viable alternative to the seemingly failing capitalist system. Most of all, Stalin basked in the moral superiority which came with the sure knowledge that the Red Army was largely responsible for the destruction of Hitler's land forces. In the run up to Yalta, Stalin was riding the crest of a wave, or at least that is how it seemed.

The Yalta Conference was held in February 1945 in the Livadia Palace in the Crimea. The sun shone bright on the former resort of the tsars referred to by Churchill as the 'Riviera of Hades'. This conference marked the high point of cooperation between the members of the Grand Alliance. Stalin agreed to enter the war against Japan within three months of the defeat of Nazi Germany. However, there were also major sticking points regarding the future political direction of post-war Poland and the issue of German war reparations. These issues served to uncover the ideological and political differences that had been papered over for so long in order to maintain the unity of the wartime alliance. After Yalta, the key to cooperation lay mostly in the genuine rapport shared by Roosevelt and Stalin. Following Roosevelt's death on 12 April 1945, his vice-president Harry Truman was sworn into office. Truman was an altogether different proposition than his predecessor. Prone to less than subtle deliberations, Truman saw matters in more simple terms, regarding Stalin's actions as those of a bully intent on imposing his political system on Eastern Europe.

To the general public in America and Great Britain, Stalin was known by the affectionate title of 'Uncle Joe'. This appellation gave the impression that the Soviet leader was a genial, benevolent figure whose life and work was devoted to serving the interests of his people. In reality, nothing could have been further from the truth, as behind his somewhat unremarkable and benign appearance lay almost unfathomable levels of viciousness and jealousy which arose from his love of power. Wearied to near exhaustion by the demands of war, Stalin was nonetheless determined to ensure his own survival by bringing about the total defeat of Germany. Once this external threat had been erased, he could then concentrate on the elimination of those who had become either real or perceived political threats at home. Above all, he wanted time to rebuild his shattered state. As such, the last thing he wanted at this time was another war. The engine of history would take care of the capitalist nations in due course.

Stalin firmly believed that time was on his side, as the greed of the rapacious Americans and British would enter into conflict with each other as they sought to dominate world trade. All he had to do was sit back and wait for the inevitable clash which would result in the destruction, or the fatal weakening of these rival powers. Thereafter, a rejuvenated Soviet state would step in to claim the spoils. His thinking was clearly influenced by Marxist–Leninist ideology which argued that capitalist states could only cooperate for a limited period as their self-interests would inevitably come to the fore sooner or later. Stalin remained stubbornly wedded to the dialectics of Marxist–Leninist ideology. In October 1952, his assertions regarding the inevitability of a clash between competing capitalist states were published in *Pravda*:

> Some comrades affirm that in consequence of the development of international conditions after the Second World War, wars among capitalist countries have ceased to be inevitable ... These comrades are mistaken. They see the external appearances which glitter on the surface but they fail to see those profound forces which, though at present operating imperceptibly, will nevertheless determine the course of events ... It is said that the contradictions between capitalism and socialism are greater than the contradictions between the capitalist countries. Theoretically this is of course true. It is true not only now, at the present time, but it was also true before the Second World War. And this the leaders of the capitalist countries did more or less understand. Yet the Second World War began not with a war against the USSR, but with a war among the capitalist countries.

> After the First World War it was believed that Germany had been finally put out of action ... Yet in spite of this Germany revived and rose to her feet as a great power ... It is typical in this regard that none other than Britain and the USA should have helped Germany to revive economically and to raise her economic war potential. Of course, through helping Germany to revive, they intended to direct her against the USSR. However, Germany directed her forces in the first place against the Anglo–French–American bloc. When Hitler attacked the USSR, The Anglo–French–American bloc not only failed to join with Hitler, but, on the contrary, were obliged to enter into a coalition with the USSR. Consequently, the capitalist countries struggle for markets and their desire to crush their competitors turned out to be actually stronger than the contradictions between the camp of capitalism and the camp of socialism ... It follows that the inevitability of wars amongst the capitalist countries remains.

It would be easy to dismiss Stalin's assertions as wishful thinking. However, his views have some credibility in that the First World War was essentially a war amongst capitalist states. It should also not be forgotten that the unwelcome interventions by foreign powers during the 1918–20 Civil War left a lasting impression on the Soviet body-politic. There were those, including Stalin himself who thought that the capitalist powers would intervene again in Soviet affairs, given the chance to do so.

On 20 April 1945, the new president met with his Moscow ambassador Averell Harriman, secretary of state Edward Stettinus Jr., under-secretary Joseph C. Grew and Charles 'Chip' Bohlen. Over the previous week, Truman had stayed up late every night studying the minutes of the Yalta negotiations in the map room of the White House. He had been kept woefully ill-informed by his predecessor. However, thanks to his own efforts, he was now almost up to speed on the state of current affairs and international relations. Ambassador Harriman used the meeting both as a conduit to pour out his frustrations concerning relations with the Soviet Union and as an opportunity to appraise the president about some 'unpleasant facts' concerning Stalin's intentions in Eastern Europe. Bohlen's memorandum of the meeting provides a clear picture of how the tone set by Roosevelt for the conduct of US relations with the Soviet Union was to harden considerably:

> ... At the President's request Ambassador Harriman made a brief report on his opinion of the present problems facing the United States in relation to the Soviet Union. He said that he thought the Soviet Union had two policies which they thought they could successfully pursue at the same

> time—one, the policy of cooperation with the United States and Great Britain, and the other, the extension of Soviet control over neighbouring states through unilateral action. He said that he thought our generosity and desire to cooperate was being misinterpreted in Moscow by certain elements around Stalin as an indication that the Soviet Government could do anything it wished without having any trouble with the United States. He said that he thought the Soviet Government did not wish to break with the United States since they needed our help in order to reduce the burden of reconstruction and that he felt we had nothing to lose by standing firm on issues that were of real importance to us ... The President said that he was not afraid of the Russians and that he intended to be firm but fair since in his opinion the Soviet Union needed us more than we needed them ... He said that only on a give and take basis could any relations be established.
>
> Ambassador Harriman said that in effect what we were faced with was a 'barbarian invasion of Europe', that Soviet control over any foreign country did not mean merely influence on their foreign relations but the extension of the Soviet system with secret police, extinction of freedom of speech, etc., and that we had to decide what should be our attitude in the face of these unpleasant facts. He added that he was not pessimistic and felt that we could arrive at a workable basis with the Russians but that this would require a reconsideration of our policy and the abandonment of the illusion that for the immediate future the Soviet Government was going to act in accordance with the principles which the rest of the world held to in international affairs....

It could be argued that the assumption made by Harriman and Truman that the Soviet Union would be dependent on aid from the US was as big a miscalculation as that made by Stalin regarding future American policy. With neither side really understanding the other, the scene was set for a complete break in relations and the beginnings of the Cold War.

Late in the afternoon of 23 April 1945, Truman met with Stalin's foreign minister Vyacheslav Molotov in the White House to discuss the political impasse regarding the formation of a legitimate government in Poland. As expected, Molotov refused to move on the issue of non-Communist Poles being included in the new government. Indeed, Moscow had given full support to the sixteen Communist members of the provisional Polish government, while agitating against the remaining nine who were regarded as deeply suspect by Stalin. Agitation was soon superseded by outright terror directed against Stanislaw Mikolajczyk's Peasant Party and the non-Communist alliance supported by London and Washington. These hard-line tactics risked a confrontation with the western powers, however Stalin was prepared to take the risk, convinced as he was that the new American president would continue with his predecessor's idealistic policies. However, Molotov's dressing-down by Truman in the White House quickly disabused him of this idea as it clearly signalled a change in the tone of political relations.

During the course of this game-changing twenty-four-minute meeting, the Soviet emissary was cut short by an exasperated president whose bargaining style was based more on hard realism than his predecessor's misplaced idealism. Later, a shocked Molotov remarked that the president, 'began talking to me in such an imperious tone'. Bohlen felt convinced that had Roosevelt still been alive he would have taken the same hard line, however he also conceded that his approach would characteristically have been 'more diplomatic and somewhat smoother'. Truman was clearly pleased with the results of the meeting, as a few days later he bragged about his pugnacity by stating that, 'I gave it to him straight. I let him have it. It was a straight one–two to the jaw'. Hardly presidential language, but it marked what Bohlen noted was, 'Probably the first sharp words uttered during the war by an American President to a high Soviet official'. What was actually said at this meeting has been much embellished over the years, not least by Truman himself. However, as a turning point in US–Soviet relations, its importance cannot be overstated.

3

Nuclear Politics

The forthcoming meeting of the 'Big Three' at Potsdam did not worry President Truman unduly. After all, he had two trump cards to play, his nation's economic power and the American monopoly in nuclear weaponry. Surely Stalin could not fail to be both impressed and overawed by both. As such, he intended to wring as many concessions as possible from the Soviet dictator. American industrial and economic might was indeed something to behold as the economy had more than doubled during the war years. The days of harsh economic tariffs were well and truly over as this powerhouse nation was now ready and able to trade on a worldwide scale. Furthermore, many former allies now looked to the US for financial relief. Bloodied and battered Britain received a three and three quarter million-dollar loan which was partially used to found the welfare state. The Soviet Union too considered tapping into this seemingly inexhaustible well of prosperity, but later pulled-out of negotiations, regarding the political cost as being unacceptable.

As for the development of the atomic bomb, while Stalin had been kept fully appraised of progress by the joint Anglo-American team, Truman was not briefed at all while serving as vice-president. On the day of his swearing-in as president, Stimson murmured some abstruse words regarding progress with the atomic project. Just under two weeks later he presented the new president with a memorandum summarising both the progress made with the weapon and the specialist's prognoses concerning future development and proliferation. Truman listened as Stimson explained that the only other nation capable of producing a nuclear weapon 'within the next few years' was the Soviet Union. The president was somewhat assured by reassuring words from his closest foreign policy advisor James Byrnes who opined that the atomic bomb 'might well put us in a position to dictate our own terms at the end of the war'. The genie was well and truly out of the bottle. The question was, what political advantage could be gained from the nuclear monopoly while it lasted?

Alerted to the possibility that Nazi Germany might be developing nuclear weapons and that his western Allies were most probably doing the same, Stalin had authorised a small-scale Soviet atomic project in 1942. His concerns were not without justification, as on 12 October 1941, a group of scientists met in Moscow to discuss the possibility of nuclear weapons development. The following day, scientist Pyotr Leonidovich Kapitsa's considered views were quoted in *Pravda*. Kapitsa's comments made startling reading:

> ... Explosive materials are one of the basic weapons of war ... But recent years have opened up new possibilities—the use of atomic energy. Theoretical calculations show that if a contemporary powerful bomb can, for example, destroy an entire quarter of a town, then an atomic bomb, even a fairly small one, if it is released, would be able to destroy a large capital city of several million people.

Kapitsa's comments, were no doubt of special interest to Soviet scientist Georgy Flerov, who along with fellow scientist Yulii Khariton had come to the realisation two years previously that the fission of atoms could produce weapons of extraordinary power. Flerov had previously worked under the supervision of Igor Kurchatov in a laboratory in Voronezh. His former boss was placed in charge of the Soviet atomic development programme; however it was not until March 1943 that he was allowed access to data transmitted by spy networks. Indeed, this store of priceless information had been sitting in General Fyodor Golikov's (head of the General Staff Secret Service) safe since late 1941. During this time, not a single Soviet scientist had been summoned by the security services to assess the worth of data which indicated that uranium based weapons could be developed by the Anglo-Americans within two years. The materials, particularly those sent by Klaus Fuchs (atomic scientist working on the Anglo-American nuclear project) and John Cairncross (secretary to War Cabinet member Lord Hankey) were of such a technical nature that they were beyond the understanding of the security services. Soviet paranoia meant that their much-delayed dissemination of intelligence cost the atomic research project dearly. Could the Allies be attempting to draw them into a scientific *cul-de-sac* which would weaken the Soviet economy by engaging in expensive and ultimately fruitless research? Such was the thinking of the secret service chiefs; however the scientific community knew better.

Kurchatov had come to the fore after a security check of senior scientists gathered in Moscow for a consultation meeting in the autumn of 1942 revealed that very few of them were members of the Communist Party. Furthermore, it appeared that those who were members of the party were somewhat pessimistic about the success of the project. In a note dated 9 July 1971, Molotov looked back on how he went about selecting a suitable scientist to lead the project:

> We were engaged on this work from 1943, and it was my job to find the man who could make a reality of the atomic bomb. The Chekhists gave me a list of trustworthy physicists upon whom it was possible to rely, and I chose. I called Kapitsa to me, the academician. He said that we were not ready for this, and the atomic bomb was not a weapon for this war, but something for the future. We asked Joffe. He also replied somehow unclearly. Shortly, we came around to Kurchatov, who was the youngest and least known. I summoned him, we talked, and he made a favourable impression on me. But he said that he was still very vague about the task. Then I decided to give him the materials of our secret service—the secret agents had done a very important job. For several days, Kurchatov sat in my room in the Kremlin going through these materials.

Finally, Molotov asked Kurchatov what he thought of the materials, 'Wonderful. Just what we are lacking' he replied. While Kurchatov was not allowed to share this information with his colleagues, he nonetheless worked diligently, not surprisingly earning a reputation for extraordinary foresight in the process. Still suspicious of an Anglo-American trap, Stalin refused to give the project top priority until his spy network was able to provide firm evidence that the nuclear weapons project undertaken in America was not a scientific dead-end, but a viable proposition. Meanwhile, at the Los Alamos facility, the Anglo-American Manhattan project continued to make good progress. Indeed, impending atomic realities led some scientists to begin expressing qualms about the development of nuclear weapons.

A group of scientists led by Leo Szilard approached Truman following the defeat of Nazi Germany. Szilard, who was one the founders of the Manhattan Project now began to question 'the wisdom of testing bombs and using bombs'. His greatest fear was that of nuclear proliferation as he was convinced that it was only a matter of time before Stalin had his own nuclear weapon. While not granted an audience with Truman, Szilard did get to speak with his advisor James Byrnes on 28 May 1945. The meeting proved something of a disaster for Szilard as he suggested that politicians were not qualified to decide on the future of nuclear weapons research.

Byrnes bridled at his visitor's somewhat pompous remarks, later recalling that, 'His general demeanour and his desire to participate in policy-making made an unfavourable impression on me'. Byrnes was convinced that the Soviets were at least a decade away from producing a viable weapon of their own; moreover, that in the interim, the American nuclear monopoly should be used to full effect in bringing the increasingly recalcitrant Soviet dictator to heel.

On 31 May, Stimson chaired a meeting of senior military personnel and leading scientists at the Pentagon. The aim of the meeting was to discuss and agree on a strategy for the deployment of the atomic bomb against Imperial Japan. Prior to the meeting, leading physicist Arthur Compton had circulated a memorandum amongst those slated to attend in which he forthrightly put forward his concerns, and those of his colleagues:

> The use of the atomic bomb against Japan is more a political than a military question because it introduces the question of mass slaughter, really for the first time in history. Essentially, the question of the use to be made of the new weapon carries much more serious implications than the introduction of poison gas. This whole question may well have received the broad study it demands. I merely mention it as one of the urgent problems that have bothered our men because of its many ramifications and humanitarian implications.

While the idea of using the atomic bomb as a terror weapon was anathema to Stimson, he understood the inevitability of its usage. Was not the bomb simply just another weapon, albeit one with greater potency than any other before it? Compton's preference was to keep the genie trapped within the bottle. Later, he wrote that, 'Throughout the morning's discussion, it seemed a foregone conclusion that the bomb would be used'. The inevitability of the bomb's usage was lost on Compton. Yet he had been correct about the use of the weapon being a political rather than a military question. The American public would not tolerate the very high casualty rates sustained in the fighting against Japan for much longer. The war had to be brought to an end. The atomic bomb provided the means.

The nuclear monopoly also provided tantalising political possibilities which both Truman and his advisor Byrnes were willing to exploit while the going was good. Echoing the president's views, Byrnes rejected calls by the Army Chief of Staff, General Marshall, and head of the Los Alamos Laboratory, Robert Oppenheimer, for the sharing of technical data with the Soviet Union. He also rejected the idea of a publicly announced demonstration of the bomb designed to overawe the Japanese as there was no absolute guarantee that it would actually work. Those present at the meeting bowed to the inevitable. The bomb would be used, without warning against a major Japanese city.

Byrnes rushed over to the White House as soon as the two-day meeting was concluded. While not exactly representing an absolute meeting of minds, the outcome of deliberations between the politicians, military and scientific community had been more than satisfactory in Byrnes' view. The only remaining question was whether the inexperienced president would rather chance a seaborne invasion of the Japanese mainland than use the bomb. After some discussion, Truman accepted that there was no alternative, as the costly battles of Saipan, Iwo Jima and Okinawa had shown that casualties would rise exponentially the closer they got to within striking distance of Tokyo. The decision was made. All that remained to be determined was the actual target.

The initial meeting of the Target Committee took place two weeks after Truman was sworn into office. The committee concluded that, 'Hiroshima is the largest untouched target not on the 21st Bomber Command priority list. Consideration should be given to this city'. The Target Committee met several more times in order to continue their deliberations. Yet, a pattern of thought was clearly emerging. On 31 May, the Interim Committee met again to discuss amongst other things, the military and political impact of the bomb against Japan. Members discussed at length how the bomb could be deployed in order to produce the maximum psychological effect against an enemy which appeared willing to fight to the bitter end. While the minutes clearly show that the decision to drop the bomb on a major city was debated at length, the final conclusions were somewhat contradictory:

> After much discussion, concerning various types of targets and the effects to be produced, the Secretary expressed the conclusion, on which there was general agreement, that we should not give the Japanese any warning: that we should not concentrate on a civilian area: but that we should seek to make a profound psychological impression on as many of the Japanese inhabitants as possible. At the suggestion of Dr. Conant, the Secretary agreed that the most desirable target would be a vital war plant employing a large number of workers and closely surrounded by workers houses.

Civilians were therefore not to be directly targeted, but their deaths would be considered as collateral damage in an air strike designed to shock and awe the Japanese leadership and populace. First however, the atomic bomb had to be tested.

On 7 July, Truman boarded the heavy cruiser USS *Augusta* for the long journey across the Atlantic. He was due to meet with Churchill and Stalin at Potsdam to discuss the future of the post-war world and if possible, to soothe the difficulties arising between the members of the Grand Alliance. The place chosen for the conference was decided by Stalin, the date by Truman. Potsdam would give Stalin the opportunity to demonstrate that Hitler's Reich had largely been crushed by the Red Army. The timing of the conference would tie in with the testing of the atomic bomb, its success guaranteeing Truman a stronger bargaining position. On 15 July, Truman disembarked in Antwerp. He toured Berlin the following day, seeing the devastated city and what he later recalled as 'the long, never-ending procession of old men, women and children wandering aimlessly'. That very day, the world entered the nuclear age following the successful detonation of a device in the Jornada Del Muerto desert in New Mexico. The following day George C. Harrison (assistant to Stimson) sent a coded cable reporting on the success of the 'Trinity' test. It read:

> Doctor has just returned most enthusiastic and confident that the little boy is as husky as his big brother. The light in his eyes discernible from here to high hold and I could have heard his screams from here to my farm.

At Potsdam, the latest information regarding the test was passed on to Churchill directly by Truman. He instantly recognised that the success of the atomic bomb test had changed everything. In his memoirs he wrote:

> To quell the Japanese resistance man by man and conquer the country yard by yard might well require the loss of a million American lives and half that number of British—for we were resolved to share the agony. Now all this nightmare picture had vanished ... Moreover, we should not need the Russians. The end of the Japanese war no longer depended upon the pouring in of their armies ... We had no need to ask favours of them. The array of European problems could therefore be faced on their merits.

For his part, Truman felt that the successful test had transformed the military situation in the Far East, so much so that Soviet participation in the conflict was no longer needed. The race was now on between the deployment of the latest technology and the massive Soviet forces massing for the showdown with the Japanese Kwantung Army in Manchuria. Of course, Stalin had to be told about the successful test, the question was, when?

Meanwhile, in Washington, discussions concerning the deployment of the atomic bomb continued. The final selection of the target had much to do with Stimson's persuasive qualities. He argued that the ancient city of Kyoto should be spared on humanitarian, moral and cultural grounds. Truman agreed with Stimson, stating emphatically that, 'The target will be a purely military one'. Hiroshima was not quite what he had in mind, but it was an untouched compact city where the effects of a nuclear weapon dropped in anger could be both observed and interpreted. It was estimated that Hiroshima would be almost completely destroyed. The Target Committee's recommendations were based more on practicalities than Truman and Stimson's desire to retain the high moral ground in a war which was becoming more brutal by the day. The hugely expensive process of developing the atomic bomb had created a momentum which effectively superseded moral considerations. Hiroshima would be destroyed; the Japanese would be brought to their knees. Stalin could not fail to be both impressed and fearful. At least, that was the idea.

On 18 July, Churchill and Truman discussed over lunch the timing and manner of the announcement of the successful bomb test to Stalin. Truman mused, 'I think. I had best just tell him after one of our meetings that we have an entirely novel form of bomb, something quite out of the ordinary, which we think will have decisive effects upon the Japanese will to continue the war'. Churchill agreed, albeit with some deep-seated concerns as he contemplated the ever growing economic and military power of the US *vis-à-vis* the declining power of Great Britain. The nineteenth-century had belonged to the British. Unquestionably, the twentieth-century would belong to the Americans.

The ministers of the three powers that made up the Grand Alliance were already at work. In a very business-like session convened on the morning of 18 July, they chiefly talked about Germany and firstly signed-off on those matters on which the three powers were all agreed; Germany was to be disarmed and de-Nazified, war criminals were to be brought before a trials process, all discriminatory laws drawn up under Hitler's terror regime were to be scrapped; finally, a unified Germany would be occupied and be required to submit to the authority of the occupying powers (including France). However, there was no clear agreement on how a unified Germany was to be administered as the American delegation had proposed that the Germans be both allowed and encouraged to self-govern on the basis of free-and-fair local elections. Not surprisingly, Molotov baulked at this proposal. Over the next few days, the conference followed the pattern set at Yalta, when no agreement could be found on certain issues, they were simply deferred to a non-specified date in the future. This way, the widening cracks in the Grand Alliance could be papered over. At least for a while.

Meanwhile, Stimson waited for the full report on the bomb test. As he waited, he grew increasingly concerned about how it would be used

A July 1945 session of the Potsdam Conference prior to Winston Churchill's defeat at the polls. (*Wikimedia Commons*)

to bring about a Japanese surrender. He also continued to mull-over the questions of whether to inform Stalin about the bomb and how much technical information should be shared with the Soviets thereafter. However, little did Stimson realise, Truman was already several steps ahead of him in the decision-making process. Stimson's musings were terminated on the afternoon of 23 July as General Leslie Groves' test report reached Potsdam. While Groves was certainly no great wordsmith, his report nonetheless painted a startling picture of the awesome power of the atomic bomb:

> ... The test was successful beyond the most optimistic expectations of anyone. Based on the data which it has been possible to work up to date, I estimate the energy generated to be in excess of the equivalent of 15,000 to 20,000 tons of TNT; and this is a conservative estimate. Data based on measurements which we have not yet been able to reconcile would make the energy release several times the conservative figure. There were tremendous blast effects, for a brief period there was a lightning effect within a radius of 20 miles equal to several suns in midday; a huge ball of fire was formed which lasted for several seconds. This ball mushroomed and rose to a height of over ten thousand feet before it dimmed. The light from the explosion was seen clearly at

> Albuquerque, Santa Fe, Silver City, El Paso and other points generally to about 100 miles. Only a few windows were broken although one was some 125 miles away. A massive cloud was formed which surged and billowed upward with tremendous power, reaching the sub stratosphere at an elevation of 41,000 feet, 36,000 feet above ground, in about five minutes, breaking without interruption through a temperature inversion at 17,000 feet which most of the scientists thought would stop it.

Truman was delighted by the test results, as he now knew that in the game of nuclear poker he intended to play, he held all the aces. How these aces were to be played was the issue, as so far demands for free elections in the Balkans and in Poland had either fallen on deaf ears or had been adroitly sidestepped by Stalin and Molotov.

After a particularly difficult and combative session on 24 July, Truman casually sauntered over to where Stalin was sitting. Churchill knew what was going to happen and was determined to catch not just every word, but also the Soviet Dictator's reaction. Speaking through Vladimir Pavlov (Stalin's interpreter), Truman casually stated that America now possessed 'a weapon of unusual destructive force'. Equally casually, Stalin replied, 'Glad to hear it. I hope you will make good use of it against the Japanese'. Churchill later recalled the encounter, stating:

> I was sure that Stalin had no idea of the significance of what he was being told ... If he had had the slightest idea of the revolution in world affairs which was in progress his reactions would have been obvious.

The 'Trinity' nuclear test.

> Nothing would have been easier than for him to say, 'Thank you so much for telling me about your new bomb. I of course have no technical knowledge. May I send my expert in these nuclear sciences to see your expert tomorrow morning?' But his face remained gay and genial and the talk between these two potentates soon came to an end. As we were waiting for our cars, I found myself near Truman. 'How did it go?' I asked. 'He never asked a question', he replied.

Both Churchill and Truman had completely underestimated Stalin. His apparent indifference was nothing but a ploy. Indeed, thanks to his spy network, he knew considerably more about the Manhattan Project than the American President. Later that evening, Stalin conferred with Molotov about Truman's disclosure. Molotov reacted decisively by saying, 'We'll have to talk it over with Kurchatov and get him to speed things up'. The nuclear arms race was now under way.

4

Potsdam Viewpoints

Viewpoint (A1): Cecilienhof Palace (Am Neuen Garten, 45–47, Potsdam)

The Potsdam Conference

On the morning of 25 July, the Big Three posed for the press photographers gathered at the Cecilienhof Palace. Truman appeared both relaxed and confident. His gaze was fixed on Stalin while they shook hands. These two men were unquestionably political colossi controlling colossal states, albeit by very different means. Meanwhile, Churchill looked distinctly uneasy. That morning he had awoke in a depressed state following a vivid dream which foretold his own demise. He recounted the particulars of the dream to an aide:

> I dreamed that life was over. I saw—it was very vivid—my dead body under a white sheet on a table in an empty room. I recognised my bare feet projecting from under the sheet. It was very life-like ... Perhaps this is the end.

In political terms, it was the end. The Labour landslide on 5 July was a massive shock to both Churchill personally and the Conservative Party. The 12 per cent national swing against Churchill was achieved by a positive campaigning strategy based around the slogan.'Let us face the future'. That future promised full employment, a tax-funded health service and a cradle to the grave welfare state. While voters had great respect for Churchill's wartime record, it was clear to many that he was yesterday's man, a political anachronism in a fast changing social and political landscape.

Defeat at the polls was almost matched by defeat at the conference. Churchill had achieved nothing at Potsdam, as he later lamented, 'A formidable body of questions on which there was disagreement piled upon the shelves'. Within a few days of Churchill's departure from Potsdam, the new prime minister, Clement Attlee, accompanied by Ernest Bevin, his pugnacious foreign secretary would arrive.

Attlee faced an almost impossible task in that Churchill was a difficult act to follow. To many in the British delegation, Attlee seemed a cold fish, one singularly lacking in Churchill's bonhomie and pathos. Stalin never warmed to Attlee and indeed seemed to be merely going through the motions during the later stages of the conference. One American diplomat noted that, 'After Churchill left and Attlee and Bevin returned, Stalin lost all interest. He enjoyed the give and take with Churchill across the table'. In truth, both Stalin and Truman were becoming increasingly weary of the seemingly never-ending negotiations. Neither saw Britain as a determining factor in the new world order. The Big Three had effectively become the Big Two.

Design and architectural features

The Cecilienhof Palace was designed by noted architect, painter, publicist and politician Paul Schultze-Naumburg. Work on the palace commenced in 1913 and was due to be completed two years later. The exterior design

The reconstituted 'Big Three' at Potsdam. (*Wikimedia Commons*)

was a mixture of gothic and traditional English country house styles. The interior of the residence boasted extensive wood panelling which ensured that the smoking room, music salon and cruise liner style cabin room were both simple but elegant. After Germany's defeat in 1918, Schultze-Naumberg became a leading voice among those advocating for traditional architectural and artistic forms. In 1930, he joined the Nazi Party, after which he became a leading critic of modernism. He compared modern architecture and art with the symptoms of sickness and moral degeneration. His ideas on traditionalism were later enthusiastically taken up by Hitler and Goebbels, making him a significant figure in the future shaping of Nazi culture.

Building work was delayed because of the war situation, and it was not until 1917 that the Crown Prince and his wife Cecile moved into the residence. During the Weimar period, the Crown Prince became politically active, though his ambitions were curtailed by his father's refusal to let him stand against Hindenburg in the 1932 presidential elections. Following this setback, he became an enthusiastic supporter of Hitler. However, his enthusiasm was somewhat dampened by the so-called 'Night of the Long Knives'. He then withdrew from politics completely. Nonetheless, an approach was later made by members of the military who hoped to unseat Hitler. The Crown Prince refused their entreaties, but this did not save him from being kept under surveillance by the Gestapo. Both he and his wife continued to live quietly in the residence until they were forced to flee from the approaching Red Army in 1945.

The Cecilienhof Palace.

The Cecilienhof Palace is closed to visitors on Mondays.
There is a café on site. Café Cecile is located in the courtyard of the residence.
April–October (open from 10:00 hrs–18: 00 hrs)
November–March (open from 10:00 hrs–17:00 hrs)
Guided tour/audio guide €8 per head.
Visitor information–Tel. 0049 3319694200
Web: info@spsg.de

Viewpoint (A2): KGB Prison Museum (Leistikowstrasse, 1, Potsdam)

In the hands of Soviet Military Counter Intelligence

It may seem strange to some, but the building which housed the KGB Prison was originally constructed for the Evangelical Ecclesiastical Benevolent Society between 1916–18. The building was home to a vicarage, a women's charity and a church newspaper. In 1945, the Soviet authorities requisitioned approximately 100 properties in the *Nauener Vorstadt* area which was then cordoned off and designated as Military Camp No 7. It was in this secure area that the KGB headquarters and KGB Prison were located.

The KGB Prison was formerly known as The Central Remand Prison for Soviet Military Counter-Intelligence and was operated by *SMERSH* (Soviet Military Counter-Intelligence). This feared organisation was more commonly referred to as 'Death to Spies' and was responsible for rounding up those involved in either real or imagined transgressions against the state. Until 1955, German prisoners accused of *Werwolf* (Nazi underground organisation) activities and alleged spies were held in the building. However, the vast majority of prisoners during the lifetime of the prison were Soviet military personnel accused of collaboration, black market activities or desertion. The prison was decommissioned during the late 1980s and afterwards was used as a storehouse. In 1994, the building was returned to its original owners, and for a few years it was leased to Amnesty International who used it as their base in Potsdam. The building was listed as a historical monument in 2004, and between 2007/2008 underwent a restoration in preparation for its conversion into a museum/ memorial site. The museum first opened to visitors in 2009. However, it was not until 2012 that a permanent exhibition was established.

Visitors to the site enter through a modern purpose-built visitor centre located on the corner of Grosse Weinmeisterstraße and Leistikowstraße. At the reception desk you will be given information about the site and instructions on how to locate the former prison block. The permanent exhibition is located on the first floor [this means second floor for US readers]. The exhibition largely consists of information panels and a few display cabinets. There are good quality English translations which enhance the overall experience. It is also possible to see a bronze relief model of Military Site No. 7 along with some memorial plaques and remnants of the original perimeter fence.

Until recently, relatively little was known about individual prisoners as the prison records were either destroyed or taken back to the former Soviet Union. However, extensive research has brought to light scores of cases which serve to underscore the terrible conditions endured by inmates. An electronic and hard-copy database of prisoners is available to visitors (currently no English translations available). However, the following cases will serve to illustrate the type of cases which resulted in imprisonment in the prison.

In 1946, two German boys (aged 15 and 16) were arrested after having failed to attend obligatory Russian language lessons. Both were briefly incarcerated in the KGB Prison before being sent to labour camps. It was not at all uncommon for German boys to be arrested, indeed the youngest prisoner was 12 years old.

On 23 March 1953, Horst Riewoldt was sentenced to death under Article 58 of the penal code for espionage and organising an underground group. The following month, the Soviet Supreme Court commuted his sentence to a term of fifteen years hard labour. Riewoldt was released after two-and-a-half years. In February 1956 he married. On his wedding day, both he and his bride escaped to the west.

One of the most interesting cases is that of Edwin Otto Bechstein who was a descendant of the founder of the famous piano manufacturer. In 1945, Bechstein was transferred from the POW cage to the KGB Prison, most probably because of his mother's associations with Hitler during the early days of the Nazi movement. Helene Bechstein née Capito first met Hitler in Berchtesgaden during 1921 through an introduction by his earliest mentor Dietrich Eckart. She then went on to be one of Hitler's main supporters, supplying him with funds and much needed advice on how to fit into polite society. Her daughter Lotte was Hitler's girlfriend during the first half of 1925. However, the relationship petered out during the summer months, and the disappointment over Hitler's refusal to marry her daughter rankled so much that she did not become a party member until 1944. On his release, Bechstein settled in the west and worked to rebuild the family business.

The museum is free to enter for individual visitors. Group bookings can be arranged by contacting the museum, the cost was €55 at the time of

writing (max. 19 people).
Tuesday–Sunday (10:00 hrs–18:00 hrs). Closed Mondays.
Tel. 0049 331 2011 540
Web: gedenkstaette-leistikowStraße.de

Viewpoint (A3): Glienicke Bridge (Glienicker Brücke, Konigstrasse, Berlin)

Design and Architectural Features

The first bridge constructed across the Havel was completed in the mid-seventeenth century. It was a relatively simple affair which was deemed adequate to meet the needs of the nobility whose hunting grounds were east of the river. In 1756, the bridge was opened up to the postal service, and soon after to the public. In 1777, the bridge was strengthened to cope with the increased traffic. However, by the early nineteenth century, the traffic between the royal residence at Potsdam and Berlin had increased to such a degree that it necessitated the building of a much larger structure. The renowned architect Karl Friedrich Schinkel was called upon to design a new bridge which would both comfortably cope with the increased road traffic and the growth of river traffic. He designed a bascule bridge (commonly referred to as a drawbridge) which was completed in 1834. By the beginning of the twentieth century more than 400 carriages and carts were crossing the bridge each day. The Prussian government decided that it was time to build a new bridge.

In 1904 a design competition was held to replace Schinkel's outdated stone and wood structure. The winning entry was submitted by The Johann Caspar Harkort Company of Duisburg. The new iron bridge was completed within three years and was inaugurated on 18 November 1907. The design of the bridge, particularly the ornamental ironwork on the Berlin side, was heavily criticised at the time as being ostentatious and outdated. In 1937, the bridge was widened (giving it an even more plump appearance) as it had been incorporated into the ambitious Reichstraße 1 road project which linked Aachen and Königsberg. The bridge was partially blown up in 1945. Rebuilding took several years, and it was not until December 1949 that it finally reopened. It was with some irony that the structure was renamed as 'The Bridge of Unity', as within four years it was closed to the public.

The Spies Who Came in from the Cold

The bridge is best known as being the site of Cold War prisoner exchanges. The most famous of these exchanges took place on the morning of 10

The author standing by the Glienicke Bridge *c.* 2014.

February 1962 when CIA pilot, Francis Gary Powers, walked across the bridge towards West Berlin and freedom. During the Geneva summit in July 1955, President Dwight D. Eisenhower proposed an 'Open Skies' plan which would effectively allow the US and the Soviet Union to monitor each other's nuclear capabilities from the air. The Soviet leader Nikita Khrushchev rejected the plan as he had been in the habit of making hollow boasts about the growing size of his nuclear arsenal. Determined to prove once and for all that the Soviet Union was not churning out nuclear missiles 'like sausages', Eisenhower authorised clandestine CIA missions using the new U-2 spy plane. This remarkable aircraft had a ceiling of 70,000 feet which would place it out of range of Soviet radar, fighters and missiles. Of course, for any measure introduced by one competing power, it is simply a matter of time before their adversaries introduce effective countermeasures. There was an element of hubris in these CIA overflights which inevitably led to catastrophe.

On 1 May 1960, Powers took off from an airfield at Peshawar in Pakistan for 'Operation Grand Slam'. This was a highly classified overflight deep into hostile airspace with the intention of gathering intelligence on Soviet submarine, missile and nuclear capabilities. Powers' flight plan took him over Tyuratam, Sverdlovsk, Kirov, Kotlas, Severodvinsk and Murmansk. Flying over the Soviet Union on a public holiday turned out to be a huge error of judgement as there was far less air traffic in the sky than usual. Hubris quickly turned to nemesis as Powers' plane was picked up on Soviet radar fifteen miles out from the border. Over Sverdlovsk, his plane came under fire from a battery of V-750 (S-75 variant) missiles. One missile scored a direct hit, causing Powers to eject before he had time to arm his planes self-destruct mechanism.

The so-called 'U-2 Crisis' was a massive embarrassment as claims that the U-2 was a weather plane were quickly debunked by the Soviet authorities. Powers stood trial in Moscow and was subsequently sentenced to three years' imprisonment plus an additional seven years' hard labour for 'Crimes against the Soviet people'. The diplomatic crisis which followed in the wake of Powers' capture and show trial scuppered any meaningful cooperation between the two superpowers. The cancellation of the Paris summit characterised how tense relations between Moscow and Washington had become. Nonetheless, Krushchev bided his time, believing that Eisenhower's successor would be more flexible. Powers' unsuccessful mission represented the nadir of U-2 operations as aircraft technology was soon superseded by satellite technology.

Powers was eventually exchanged for Colonel Rudolf Abel. Remarkably, this high-ranking Soviet intelligence officer was born at 140 Clara Street in Benwell (Newcastle's West End). His father Heinrich Fisher has been described as a 'staunch socialist' who was imprisoned by the Tsarist authorities. In 1901, he fled with his wife Lyubov, first to Germany, then to England. Their son William was born two years later. He was a talented boy who enjoyed sketching and reading. It was perhaps here in the industrial north-east of England that he later experienced his political awakening. In 1921, the Fisher family left Tyneside for the Soviet Union. William was never to return to his place of birth.

During the 1930s, Fisher worked for the Soviet Security Services in Oslo and London. Later, this talented multi linguist served in the Red Army. Following the German invasion of the Soviet Union he distinguished himself by carrying out effective deception measures while serving as a radio operator. Indeed, his operations at this time were so successful that his biographer Dr Vin Arthey referred to them as 'the most significant contribution of his career'. After the war ended, his career took an important turn following his recruitment by the security services as a foreign agent. He entered America illegally in 1948, during the period known as the 'Red-Scare' which had seen many Soviet spy networks rolled-up. Fisher, now known as Rudolf Abel (amongst other aliases) used his job as a photographic finisher as cover, while in reality managing and disseminating the intelligence gathered by Soviet agents. Much of this intelligence related to nuclear secrets, making it vital to the Soviet weapons programme.

Abel's clandestine activities were brought to an abrupt end on 21 June 1957. He had been betrayed by his colleague Reino Heyhanen, who had chosen to defect rather than accept his recall to Moscow. The price exacted by the US authorities was information on Soviet spy networks. Heyhanen complied willingly, his betrayal quickly leading to the solving of the 'Hollow Nickel Case'. Amongst those Soviet agents subsequently rounded up were Mikhail Nikolaevich Svirin and Rudolf Abel. Known as 'the agent who never cracked', Abel gave nothing away to the FBI investigators who interrogated him over a six-week period at a Federal Alien Detention Facility in Texas. Abel was subsequently put on trial at the Federal Court in New York in October 1957. Heyhanen, his former associate, was a star prosecution witness. His damming testimony led to Judge Mortimer W. Byers imposing a sentence of thirty years' imprisonment. Abel served four years of his sentence in the Atlanta State Penitentiary as Prisoner 80016-A before being released in preparation for the prisoner exchange with Powers.

There were only four more prisoner exchanges on the bridge. On 22 April 1964, the British spy Greville Wynne was exchanged for Soviet agent Konon Molody. Wynne was arguably responsible for the greatest single intelligence coup of the Cold War. During the height of the Cuban missile crisis, he was able to obtain valuable secrets about the Soviet ballistic missile programme. His informant was a certain Colonel Oleg Pekovsky who was later sentenced to death by the Soviet authorities. Pekovsky cheated the firing squad by committing suicide in prison.

The next exchange took place on 12 June 1985. Soviet agent Marian Zacharski was exchanged for twenty-five American agents. Zacharski was a highly proficient operator whose methods are still studied by the FBI today. Having befriended an engineer at the Hughes Aircraft plant, Zacharski was able to extract valuable technical information. Dubbed the 'Silicon Valley Spy' by the American press, Zacharski's intelligence haul was impressive. During his time spent posing as a salesman for a Polish export firm POLAMCO he saved his Soviet paymasters an estimated $185m by passing on details of proven technology including the F-15 Look Down–Shoot Down radar, the TOW anti-tank missile, the Phoenix air-to-air missile, and Quiet Radar. Following his return home, Zacharski worked for the Office of State Protection and the Pewex chain of hard currency shops which enabled citizens to purchase scarce consumer goods. Today, Zacharski is a revered figure in his native Poland. His 'Codes of War' book has become a key text in understanding the role of intelligence services within the context of international relations.

On 11 February 1986, the final exchange of the Cold War era took place. This particular exchange involving nine people was widely reported in the international press as it was brokered by no less personages than President Ronald Reagan and the Soviet leader Mikhail Gorbachev. Anatoly Shcharansky [Natan Sharansky] was the most prominent Soviet dissident exchanged. He had fallen foul of the Soviet authorities in 1978, having joined an international dissident group which was particularly vocal in its criticisms of Moscow. Shcharansky was arrested on espionage charges and subsequently sentenced to thirteen years' hard labour. He was later exchanged for Karl Koecher, a Soviet mole who had successfully penetrated the CIA. However, Koecher was later betrayed by either Oleg Kalugin (head of Soviet Counter-Intelligence) or Jan Fila (Soviet intelligence officer). While serving time in prison, Koecher was attacked by a fellow inmate who tried to stab him with a pair of scissors. His life was saved by a Hells Angel named Sandy Alexander who was able to disarm his assailant. Convinced that this was a CIA plot, Koecher contacted his lawyer, who managed to send his request for a prisoner exchange direct to the KGB. Vladimir Kryuchkov (Chairman of the KGB) subsequently agreed to the exchange. The US prosecutor's office was also keen for the exchange to take place as there were serious doubts about the evidence which had brought about Koecher's conviction. This final prisoner exchange is one of the most interesting, not only because of the involvement of Reagan and Gorbachev, but because it characterises many of the human elements which made up the Cold War era.

While the prisoner exchanges on the Glienecke Bridge have been the subject of much mythologising, the real stories remain so fascinating that they do not require any embellishment. The 2015 Hollywood film *Bridge of Spies* was at best a partially successful attempt to recreate the high tension which was so evocative of Cold War Berlin. In the opinion of film critic Geoffrey Macnab writing in *The Independent* (a British newspaper) the film 'evokes memories of everything from *The Third Man* to *The Spy Who Came in from the Cold*, but lacks their seediness and desperate pathos'. Notwithstanding the verdict in *The Independent, New York Times* critic Manhola Dergas considered that Spielberg's Cold War project made a searing impression in its representation of East Berlin's 'haunted faces and streets'. Having watched *Bridge of Spies*, the author can only agree with the verdict of *The Independent*.

5

'A Splendid Analysis'

Stalin's participation in the war against Japan was long regarded as inevitable in Washington. However, it was only during the last months of the war that American policymakers finally abandoned the Rooseveltian idea that the Soviet Union would be satisfied with a limited role in Manchuria. Soviet negotiations with the Kuomintang representative T. V. Soong had dragged on with little real progress. At Potsdam, the American position had been to avoid direct diplomatic action with regard to Sino–Soviet relations. Now, with the Soviet position becoming more bullish, President Truman was 'not too hopeful about the renewed talks between Soong and Stalin'. In order to safeguard American interests in China, a more direct approach was required. Two days after the atomic bomb was dropped on Hiroshima, Stalin entered the war against Japan. Direct intervention by the Americans in to Sino–Soviet relations now became a priority.

On 8 August 1945, Averell Harriman and George F. Kennan met with Stalin and Molotov in Moscow in order to discuss recent developments in the Far East theatre of operations. Harriman began the conversation by expressing his satisfaction that the Soviet Union was once again allied against the forces of nationalism and fascism. He then went on to ask Stalin what news he had of Soviet military operations in Manchuria. Stalin replied by saying that the initial assault had made good progress with forces advancing along the route of the Trans-Manchurian Railway from Gradekovo. Meanwhile, other forces were advancing in a southerly direction towards Hailar, eastwards through the mountain pass from Charar, and across the Gobi Desert towards Mukden. The Generalissimo went on to state that the advance towards Harbin and Chungchan on the central Manchrian sector was progressing well. Additional flanking forces massed along the Sakhalin border, and in the region between Khabarovsk and Blagoveshchensk would be held back until the Japanese Kwantung Army had committed itself on the central sector.

Stalin had confidently stated to Ambassador Harriman the previous year, that the war against Japan would progress more quickly following the entry of the Soviet Union into the conflict. Harriman could not resist reminding the Generalissimo of his prediction. Stalin, replied by magnanimously stating that the rapid progress being made against Japan, had been due to the successful two-pronged campaign mounted by General Macarthur and Admiral Nimitz in the Pacific theatre. Moving on to more immediate matters, Harriman asked Stalin about his thoughts on how the Japanese would react to the atomic bombing of Hiroshima. Stalin proffered the opinion that the Japanese were looking for a pretext to replace the present government with one more amenable to the idea of capitulation. The atomic bomb provided such a pretext.

The implications of Hiroshima led to a brief exchange regarding the difficulties encountered in the development process. Stalin admitted that his scientists had made only limited progress thus far. Harriman replied by stating that the Anglo American project had been hugely expensive. Both agreed that the atomic bomb could be used as a means of maintaining peace and stability as long the scientific data remained secret. Stalin's response was however nothing more than a pose, as in reality he was deeply concerned that Soviet blood expended on the battlefronts would no longer be translated into political influence. The balance had been destroyed; the actual deployment of the bomb against a strategic target in Japan was for Stalin a seismic leap in the conduct of war. 'War is barbaric, but using the A-bomb is super-barbarity', he was heard to complain after the destruction of Hiroshima.

Soviet troops had captured the Kaiser Wilhelm Institute for Physics in the Dahlem district of Berlin on 25 April 1945. While much of the institute's equipment had long since been moved to the Black Forest, Soviet technical experts were still able to requisition 250 kilograms of metallic uranium, three tons of uranium oxide, and twenty litres of heavy water. However, this important boost to Soviet nuclear research was not fully exploited until the full political implications of Hiroshima and Nagasaki became apparent. On 20 August, a special committee was formed to solve the nuclear problem in the shortest possible time. Beria quickly usurped control of nuclear matters from Molotov. His role would prove crucial as he was able to draw upon the human resources of his vast prison empire.

Beria was ably assisted by Colonel General Avaraami Zaveniagin who was a metallurgist by training. By the summer of 1945, the direction pursued by Beria and Zaveniagin had given Chief Scientist Kurchatov sufficient confidence to begin designing the first large plutonium reactor, code-named Chelyabinsk-40. Such was the urgency of the Soviet programme, that as work proceeded on the plutonium reactor, the construction of a graphite moderated pile and an experimental radio-chemical shop was already nearing completion in Moscow's No. 2 Laboratory. On 21 August 1947, a special resolution called for the establishment of a special facility to test nuclear weapons. Kurchatov selected a remote area 160 kilometres west of the city of Semipalatinsk in Kazakhstan. Within months, military personnel began to arrive. The garrison made camp sixty kilometres east of the test site on the banks of the Irtysh River. Stalin would get his bomb. However, in the meantime, American policy-makers would continue to push their own foreign policy objectives, backed by their nuclear monopoly.

No matter how hard Soviet scientists worked, it would take time to produce a viable atomic weapon. In the meantime, his policy was to deny the Americans a dominating position in establishing the new world order by taking an increasingly uncompromising position with regard to pursuing Soviet objectives. In late 1945, he made his position clear by stating to his political staff that, 'It is obvious, that we cannot achieve anything serious if we begin to give in to intimidation or betray uncertainty'. Stalin's uncompromising attitude led to each crisis feeding the next one, as once Eastern Europe and Northeast Asia had been secured he turned his eyes towards Iran, Turkey, and the Eastern Mediterranean. For the Americans, the spirit of wartime cooperation had been exploited to the limit by Stalin. Now was the time for firmness.

The new hard line taken by Washington's policy-makers came simultaneously with a pressing need to understand the sources of Soviet behaviour. A Treasury Department request for opinion regarding Soviet policy produced the required information in the form of George F. Kennan's 'Long Telegram'. Kennan was a junior, but well-respected Foreign Service officer based in the American Embassy in Moscow. His hastily composed 8,000 word telegram was a genuine attempt to explain the Soviet enigma. Kennan was careful to avoid referencing Stalin directly, instead focusing on the government, the people, and the ideology of Communism.

Kennan's telegram consisted of five sections which together explained the sources of Soviet behaviour. The first section considered the basic features of the post-war Soviet outlook. In this section, Kennan emphasised that the post-war Soviet outlook was not shared by the majority of the population but was instead largely a product of propaganda. The basis of this propaganda was a rhetoric which strongly argued that capitalist states were not harmonious by design, and that their internal conflicts would inevitably evolve into general wars which would directly or indirectly

George Kennan, author of the *Long Telegram c.* 1947. (*Wikimedia Commons*)

affect the Soviet Union. In order to avoid being embroiled in capitalist discord, Soviet propaganda should exploit weaknesses by encouraging revolutionary action. In the second section, Kennan argued that insecurity formed the root of Soviet intransigence. This insecurity was deep-seated, having long been a feature of the Tsarist era:

> At the bottom of the Kremlin's neurotic view of world affairs is a traditional and instinctive Russian sense of insecurity. For Russian rulers have invariably sensed that their rule was relatively archaic, and unable to stand comparison or contact with political systems of Western countries.

In essence, Kennan was explaining that in order to maintain control over its own citizens, the Soviet Union had to conceal the truth about the higher living standards in America. The third section looked at the projection of the Soviet outlook on an official level. In this section, Kennan stated that the Kremlin's ultimate aim was to further the spread of Communism, while simultaneously degrading the power of American institutions. The fourth section focused on the projection of the Soviet outlook on an unofficial level. This section demonstrated the degree to which Communist organisations had penetrated every aspect of society in the Soviet Union. Kennan postulated that infiltration and espionage by Communist agents was inevitable as Stalin's policymakers in Moscow were intent on spreading their doctrine on American soil. The final section drew together Kennan's insights into practical deductions from the standpoint of American policy. Kennan strongly articulated that co-existence was no longer possible, and that conflict was inevitable:

> In Summary, we have a political force committed fanatically to the belief that with the United States there can be no permanent *modus vivendi*, that it is desirable and necessary that the internal harmony of our society be disrupted, our traditional way of life be destroyed, the internal authority of our state be broken, if Soviet power is to be secure.

Kennan concluded by arguing that the Soviet Union would use a combination of both direct and indirect means to undermine America. Therefore, the only sensible policy that Washington could adopt to forestall Soviet intentions was one of vigorous containment.

While Kennan's telegram set into motion a new direction for American foreign policy, his reasoning was somewhat flawed in that he appears to have been blithely unaware of the depth of Soviet security concerns. These concerns were the justifiable result of having twice been invaded by Germany in 1914 and 1941. The nation had only recently emerged victorious but battered after a long and bloody war against the forces of Nazism. American nuclear diplomacy at Potsdam, and Macarthur's insistence that the Soviet Union had no part in the occupation of Japan further increased anxiety in the Kremlin.

With his ambitions in South East Asia stymied, Stalin turned his full attention towards Europe, and Germany in particular. The Generalissimo aspired to unite Germany, but lacked the means to achieve his goal. There was no clear strategy for winning over the German people. Indeed, the prospect of co-operation seemed impossible following the havoc wrought by the Soviet *fronkovki*, the mass arrests by the secret police, the uncoordinated and destructive dismantling of industry, the cession of German land to Poland, and the retention of German prisoners of war. However, in the spring of 1946, a directive from the Soviet Military Administration in Germany calling for the establishment of a single unified political party headquartered in Berlin opened up possibilities which could be exploited by the Propaganda Department.

Soviet propaganda in Germany was overseen by Colonel Sergei Tiulpanov, arguably Stalin's most effective ideologue in Berlin. Tiulpanov was amiable, spoke fluent German and was a confirmed Bolshevist who was a strong advocate of the Sovietisation of Eastern Germany. When he met with Berlin's leading Social Democrats, he was both gregarious and solicitous. Tiulpanov's promises of cars, winter fuel and luxury food items turned many of them into tame politicians, all too ready to acquiesce to the formation of working groups and committees whose declared aim was to pave the way for a formal union between the Social Democrats and the Communist Party of Germany. Those politicians not taken in by Tiulpanov's charm were later arrested and imprisoned.

On 1 March 1946, a conference was convened at Berlin's Admiralspalast in order to arrange a vote of Social Democrats on the proposed merger. A ballot was subsequently arranged for the last day of the month. On the day of the vote, Soviet troops in East Berlin stepped in to seal the ballot boxes less than thirty minutes after the polls had opened. Voters waiting patiently outside were quickly dispersed. Meanwhile, in the Allied sector of the city, voting went ahead uninterrupted, resulting in a crushing defeat for the merger proposal. A second proposal for a 'working alliance' met with a more favourable response. Little did they know that by electing to work with the Communists, they had effectively sealed their own fate.

On 20 October, the population cast their votes in the City Council elections for Greater Berlin. Predictably, the turnout was high, at just over ninety-two per cent. The Soviet authorities and the German Communists refrained from interfering in the conduct of the elections, but made determined and unscrupulous efforts behind the scenes to skew the results in their favour. In the event, the Marxist inspired Social Unity Party failed to prevent a Social Democratic majority in all of Greater Berlin's twenty boroughs. Indeed, the Marxist failure at the polls was so complete that they even failed to secure more than one-third of the vote in the working-class borough of Weissensee.

Following their clear-cut victory in Berlin, the Social Democrats could legitimately claim to be the principal party of the working-class in Berlin. The Social Democrat, Otto Ostrowski was subsequently elected as Berlin's lord mayor. Seventeen other Social Democrats were elected to administer the various departments of the city council. After much procrastination by the Soviet Kommandatura, all but two members received official approval. However, the ambitions of the Social Democrats were stymied by the Soviet authorities who prevented the newly elected department heads from removing their Communist deputies, many of whom had been in post since May/June 1945. Realising that his administration could not function under such conditions, Ortrowski entered into secret negotiations with the Social Unity Party. When the Social Democrat leadership learned of Ortrowski's overtures, they forced him to resign. The city assembly then elected Ernst Reuter as lord mayor. The Soviet authorities quickly rejected Reuter on account of his anti-Communist leanings. Luise Schroeder, who had been installed as acting lord mayor following Ortrowski's resignation remained in post until new elections were held in December 1948. By this time, Berlin was an officially divided city.

6

Sinews of Peace

Having been voted out of office by the British people in July 1945, Churchill was increasingly feeling that events were leaving him behind. As such, he was looking for a suitable opportunity to step back onto the world stage. That opportunity was provided by the American President, who enthusiastically endorsed an invitation for him to speak from Westminster College by stating, 'This is a wonderful school in my home state. Hope you can do it. I'll introduce you'. Churchill did not hesitate, gratefully taking up the invitation. As a former statesman, there were few restrictions on what he could say. As such, Westminster College provided Churchill with a golden opportunity to publicly voice his concerns about Soviet aggression and expansionist tendencies in Eastern Europe. His speech essentially had two themes, that the Soviets would use all means short of war to spread their doctrine, and that only a united stand by America and Great Britain could force Stalin to reconsider his expansionist policies.

Press coverage of Churchill's speech was extensive, and largely critical, *The New York Times* opining that he had painted 'a dark picture of post-war Europe'. An editorial by Walter Lipmann in *The Wall Street Journal* was even more damning, referring to the speech as an 'almost catastrophic blunder'. The newspapers reflected the popular mood, as large sections of the public still regarded the Soviets as 'our gallant ally'. Sensing the public's mood, Truman disingenuously stated that he had not seen a draft copy of Churchill's speech. When asked to comment by reporters, he lamely replied, 'No comment'. Truman's equivocations reflected a certain degree of bewilderment, as he seemed incapable of formulating a clearly defined policy towards the Soviets. Such a policy would develop in time, once the political implications of Kennan's telegram had been fully digested by his administration.

Churchill and Truman *en route* to Fulton Missouri for the 'Iron Curtain' speech. (*Wikimedia Commons*)

Stalin reacted to Churchill's theatrical rhetoric by using some striking metaphors of his own in a strongly worded interview published by *Pravda* on 12 March 1946. By aiming a series of poisonous barbs at Churchill, Stalin was able to deflect attention away from his own ambitions in Eastern Europe. The interview portrayed Churchill as an out-of-touch yesterday's man, intent on starting a military conflict with the Soviet Union. Stalin stated that the former leader's 'tragedy' was that he was 'an inveterate Tory' who could not grasp the simple truth that Communism represented the new wave in international politics. By sounding the alarm at Westminster College, Churchill had become a Don Quixote figure 'with his cries about totalitarianism, tyranny, and policing'. This type of rhetoric found a receptive audience at home. Indeed, by adroitly casting Churchill as a warmonger, Stalin was able to convincingly state the case that the Americans and British were dangerous imperialists.

While the Soviet population could be manipulated by clever words, the millions of Germans living in Soviet occupied areas were harder to convince. Few of these people thought that they had a stake in Soviet success, or in a Soviet-sponsored future. Conditions in Eastern Germany had hardly improved since the end of the war. Berlin was frozen in a condition of wartime destruction. The pillaging of Berlin's factories had weakened the economy to such an extent that the social fabric was severely weakened, and the German Communists found themselves alienated. Despite Stalin's change to a policy of reconciliation in mid-1946, the rot had set in, one characterised by the dismal failure of German Communists at the polls, and the migration of skilled workers to the Allied zones. For Stalin, these setbacks served to highlight the perceived threat of a united and economically resurgent Germany.

In Berlin, the new policy of reconciliation quickly gave way to one of repression as the population were faced with the dilemma of aligning themselves either with the West or with the Communists. On 12 March 1947, Tiulpanov dispatched a secret message to Moscow outlining the issues:

> There is a vigorous discussion within the population of Berlin over whether the Germans will remain a single country or be broken into pieces. At the same time, there is a growing fear that Germany could be divided up due to the opposing political views and ambitions of the Allies.

The Soviet authorities anticipated the break-up of Germany by demanding loyalty. Writing in the *Tägliche Rundschau*, Tiulpanov wrote that, 'It is very clear that, in a zone occupied by the troops of a socialist country, only truly democratic parties stand a chance of further development'. Behind these words lay an implied threat, toe the line or face the consequences. Indeed, the consequences would be severe—the Soviet authorities were experts in treating their real or perceived political adversaries with the utmost ruthlessness.

By March 1948, 6,455 people had 'disappeared' in Berlin alone. Many were political prisoners, including Social Democrats, Christian Democrats, and even some German Communists whose role as a 'useful idiot' had come to an end. As the prisons filled, some prominent voices articulated their concerns. In April 1948, the usually compliant Walter Ulbricht complained to Tiulpanov about the effect that the critical food situation, the continuing dismantling of factories, and the disappearance of party members was having on morale. In a report compiled in November 1948, Major General Ivan Kolesnitchenko wrote:

> The disappearance of people as a result of the activities of our operative sectors is already the cause of great concern within the German population. I would venture to say that this approach by our security

> officials elicits severe anti-Soviet propaganda and hatred of us among the Germans.

Despite these concerns, the Soviet understanding of what kind of domestic political order was required in Germany became increasingly characterised by the application of totalitarian ruthlessness.

At a meeting with leading German Communists in December 1948, Stalin criticised them for their 'premature' efforts to construct a Socialist workers utopia by saying, 'Socialism must be approached by zigzags, not directly ... Conditions in Germany dictate a more cautious policy'. While the German Communists were in theory granted a degree of discretion from adherence to strict Marxist–Leninist orthodoxy, the reality was different. Soviet political officers encouraged the German Communists to follow similar organisational and behavioural patterns to those implemented in the Soviet Union. Those who dissented continued to 'disappear'.

7

Strategic Philanthropy

By early 1947, American officials were becoming increasingly concerned about Soviet behaviour. These concerns centred on the pressure being put on Turkey over the control of the Black Sea Straits, attempts to pressure the Iranians into granting oil concessions, a refusal to accept the Baruch plan for the international control over nuclear energy, and apparent support for Greek Communists. In March 1947, the impoverished British government announced that they no longer had the resources to support the Greek government against the Communist threat. The Truman administration proved willing to fill the void. However, limiting economic assistance to Greece looked too much like supporting British imperial interests. Therefore, in an address to Congress on 12 March 1947, Truman announced a doctrine that would aid all democracies resisting Communist minorities. This doctrine effectively reoriented American foreign policy. Germany in particular was being looked at through a new perspective, Kennan noting that, 'To talk about the recovery of Europe and to oppose the recovery of Germany is nonsense. People have to have both, or they can have neither'.

On 25 November, the Council of Foreign Ministers met for the fifth time in London. The attendees were unable to establish any common ground, and the meeting subsequently broke up with each side condemning the other. In a report on the meeting dated 19 December, Secretary of State Marshall wrote:

> It finally became clear that we could make no progress at this time and that there was no apparent will to reach a settlement, but only an interest in making more and more speeches intended for another audience. So I suggested that we adjourn. No real ground was lost or gained at the meeting, except that of outlines of the problems and the obstacles are

> much clearer. We cannot look forward to a unified Germany at this time. We must do the best we can in the area where our influence can be felt.
>
> All must recognise that the difficulties to be overcome are immense ... There is another and I think more fundamental reason for the frustration we have encountered in our endeavour to reach a realistic agreement for a peace settlement. In the war struggle, Europe was in a large measure shattered. As a result, a political vacuum was created, and until this vacuum has been filled by the restoration of a healthy European community, it does not appear possible that paper agreements can lead to a lasting peace. It is for this very reason that I think we encountered such complete opposition to almost every proposal the western powers agreed upon. The Soviet Union has recognised the situation in its frank declaration of hostility and opposition to the European Recovery Program ...
>
> The issue really is clear-cut, and I feel that there can be no settlement until the coming months demonstrate whether or not the civilisation of Western Europe will prove vigorous enough to rise above the destructive effects of the war and restore a healthy society. Officials of the Soviet Union and the leaders of the Communist parties openly predict that this restoration will not take place ... Now until the result of this struggle becomes clearly apparent, there will continue to be a very real difficulty to resolve, even on paper, agreed terms for a treaty of peace. The situation must be stabilised. Western nations at the very least must be firmly established on a basis of government and freedoms that will preserve all that has been gained in the past centuries by these nations and all that their cooperation promises in the future.

In a radio address to the American people, Marshall went even further, stating that, 'If the Americans cannot get Soviet support for their policy towards Germany, then they would go it alone in the Western zones.

The initial Soviet response to the Marshall Plan was wholly negative, an article in *Pravda* on 16 June describing it as merely 'an extension of the Truman Doctrine'. Two weeks later, another article went even further into condemning the plan as interference in state sovereignty by stating:

> Hitherto it has been regarded as axiomatic that every nation should itself decide the question how best to ensure the restoration and improvement of its economy ... Such is the viewpoint of the Soviet Union which has more than once resisted the attempt at foreign interference in its affairs. It has been regarded as completely obvious that internal economic affairs are the sovereign affair of nations themselves and that other countries should not interfere in these internal affairs. Only on this basis is the normal development of relations between countries possible. Attempts

> at interference from without in the economic life of individual countries have never led and will never lead to positive results.

On 4 July 1947, invitations were sent out to the representatives of twenty-two European governments for a meeting in Paris to discuss their participation in the American sponsored recovery plan. Western observers were gratified to note the eager response of the Czechoslovak, Hungarian, and Polish representatives. However, the Kremlin soon began to apply pressure. The Soviets had rejected participation in the Marshall Plan due to the perceived threat of the spreading of American influence. Therefore, Stalin was determined that his satellites would not be themselves susceptible to this threat. Stalin's fear of the spread of American influence led to the division of Europe, a two-state Germany, and to Berlin becoming the crucible of the Cold War.

Prior to the forthcoming meeting of the Council of Foreign Ministers in London in late November, Soviet Deputy Foreign Minister F. Gustev sent a memorandum of recommendations to Molotov. This memorandum is a clear expression of concern at the spread of Western influence, particularly in Berlin:

> After the Council of Foreign Ministers session in Moscow, the policy of the British–American bloc for the division of Germany developed further. During this time, minor issues continued to isolate the British–American zones. United economic bodies were established in the British–American zone, their structure enabling them to quickly transform into Western German federal political bodies.
>
> Coordinated action on decisions made at the Council of Foreign Ministers session on minor issues of the Control Council report are not being carried out in Western zones. In the last six months the Control Council could not solve any important issue regarding Germany as a whole. Practical work of joint bodies in Germany revealed that the British–American bloc strive towards eliminating any of the Soviet Union's influence on decisions on issues concerning the Western zones, and preserving and expanding British–American influence in the Soviet zone and in Berlin....
>
> The Soviet Union's democratic policy for establishing stable peace will encounter different forms of resistance from American reactionary ruling circles. The state of relations between allies—defeaters of Germany enables us to forecast that at the forthcoming Council of Foreign Ministers meeting in London we should not expect the British–American bloc to display a spirit of cooperation in implementing decisions of the Crimean and Berlin conferences. Most likely the opposite will happen: at this council of Foreign Ministers, session attempts will be made to declare the Potsdam decisions outdated and requiring replacement with

> new ones. In this case you can expect a repeat of demagogic accusations against the Soviet Union, who allegedly did not carry out these decisions.... Nowadays it becomes more and more clear that the British–American bloc is afraid of a democratic Germany and thus strives to transform it into the base of European reaction....
>
> The Soviet Union has relatively few effective tools for influencing the Anglo–Americans to carry out the obligations accepted by them in accordance with the agreements. However, it would be erroneous to underestimate the Anglo–Americans great interest in the outcome of the German question and, in particular, its interest in what is the Soviet zone of occupation.
>
> According to the occupied zones agreement, a Greater Berlin zone was to be formed where all-German organs would have been, but if Germany remains broken up without all-German organs, then there is no need to have a special zone with British, American, and French participation. The Anglo–American forces presence in the Greater Berlin zone gives them not only access to information in the Soviet zone, but also an opportunity to influence the population in the Soviet-occupied zone via their sectors in the city of Berlin....
>
> If at the forthcoming Council of Foreign Ministers session, Britain and America will not satisfy the legal requirements of the Soviet Union, in particular on reparations, on the joint control of the Ruhr, etc., perhaps the Soviet Union will have to raise the issue of abolishing the Greater Berlin zone and declare all of this territory part of the Soviet zone. Certainly, it is an extreme measure and should be used only when there would be no hope for an agreement....

At the meeting of the Council of Foreign Ministers, and at a subsequent meeting of the Allied Control Council, the Soviets rejected proposals for currency reform, as this would have inevitably led to a Western-influenced all-German state. The Allies went ahead without Soviet support, but when they attempted to extend these reforms to West Berlin, the Soviets responded quickly.

On 24 June 1948, the Soviets reacted to the Anglo–American currency reforms by blockading all routes into Berlin. Stalin's reasoning behind this rash venture remains somewhat obscure. He may have hoped to force the Allies out of their respective zones in Berlin, or he may have wished to disrupt the consolidation of these zones. At first, the Western powers feared that they would have to give in; then it became clear that a retreat from Berlin would be a prelude to a retreat from Germany. 'We are going to stay, period', thundered Truman. The British Foreign Secretary Ernest Bevin was equally resolute, stating that 'the abandonment of Berlin would mean the loss of Western Europe'. This forceful rhetoric belied the practical difficulties of supplying over two million Germans and the Allied garrisons with provisions for a protracted blockade.

While the Soviet blockade had been anticipated by Washington, no clear policy had been formulated for how to deal with it. Therefore, it was left to the commanders on the ground to respond. The first to do so was Colonel Frank Howley, who served as second-in-command to General Lucius Clay who headed the Office of Military Government. Howley took to the airwaves soon after the full blockade became apparent. Firstly, he reassured the population by stating that, 'We are not getting out of Berlin, and we are going to stay'. He then directly challenged the Soviets by saying, 'We have heard a lot about your military intentions ... If you do try to come into our sector, you'd better be well prepared. We are ready for you'. Later that day, General Clay stated to the press that, 'The Soviets cannot drive us out by an action short of war as far as we are concerned'. As no firm commitment to hold Berlin had yet been reached by Washington's policy-makers, the pronouncements made by Howley and Clay caused a certain degree of consternation on Capitol Hill. Indeed, confusion reigned for several days until Truman personally intervened to quash any further talk of a withdrawal from Berlin.

The Allies quickly implemented a counter-blockade, halting all rail traffic into East Germany from the British and American zones. This strategic move had a devastating effect on industry in the Soviet zone. At a conference held in Berlin–Karlshorst on 28 June, Soviet officials met with representatives of East German industry to discuss the effects of the counter-blockade. A declassified Central Intelligence Agency document dated 30 June provides valuable insights into these effects, their consequences, and the Soviet authority's incredible lack of foresight:

> Information has been received that a conference was held in Karlshorst on 28 June 1948 between Russian officials, headed by Marshal Sokolovsky, and German members of the German Industrial Committee. Sokolovsky opened the conference by asking the German industrialists what influence on the Eastern Zone of Germany would exist because of the blockade from the Western Zone.
>
> A German representative stated that being cut off from the West meant a complete stoppage of production in sugar refineries for lack of 50,000 metres of steel piping on order in the Western Zone; it almost meant a complete closing down of canneries since the entire raw material was received from the West; and a certain discontinuance of the Baltic fishing fleet within a short time because of lack of machinery parts. Sokolovsky evidenced a great consternation at this statement, replying that the Russians had been led to believe the East could be independent

> of the West. The German member then stated that the heavy industries, particularly the steel mills in Hennigsdorf, could not produce without the West and that other heavy industries in the Eastern Zone would be equally affected. The Russians appeared greatly shocked, and a Russian General in charge of trade and supply, said, 'We had no idea of this situation; Russia is suffering from heavy droughts and is counting on German food supplies this year. Food supplies must be maintained, come what may. If we had known this, we would not have gone so far'.
>
> During the meeting Sokolovsky stated that three possibilities were available: a). Start a war; b). Lift travel restrictions on Berlin; c). Leave entire Berlin to the West, giving them the rail line.
>
> After the meeting Tulpanov, who was also present, said that war was impossible, due to the harvest prospects and that lifting travel restrictions would make the Russians lose face. The third possibility was that the West would have to feed all of Berlin and would have more on their hands than they bargained for....

Three months earlier, the British Army of the Rhine and the Royal Air Force Transport Command had worked on a plan which anticipated the Soviet blockade. This plan gave no consideration to the civilian population of Berlin, focusing entirely on the supply of the garrison and the evacuation of family members by air. When the blockade was imposed, the practicalities of supplying the garrison appeared daunting, particularly as the political stakes were so high. The British Foreign Office assessed the situation soberly, noting:

> If the Soviet Government were to succeed in their efforts to force us out (of Berlin) in humiliating circumstances the effect would be extremely grave not only in Berlin but in Western Germany and in Europe at large. It might prove impossible for the Western powers to maintain their position at all in Western Germany, if Berlin were lost to them, except by heavily reinforcing the military forces there.

General Clay was sceptical about the British plan which he regarded as hopelessly optimistic. Clay's favoured response was to send a convoy of engineers down the autobahn to clear a route through the Soviet obstacles. The White House baulked at Clay's proposal, knowing that it could lead to a war which the American people would have no taste for. The British senior military advisors also pointed out the precarious position of the Western forces in Berlin by stating that their current position was 'militarily unsound and could not be maintained by fighting.... The Russians could squeeze us out of Berlin without themselves firing a shot'.

Having advocated a firm stance against Soviet aggression, Truman knew that any action short of war was preferable to doing nothing. The credibility of the West's position in Berlin was at stake. The plan to supply Berlin by air gained increasing credibility as there was no other practical alternative. On 25 June, George N. Shuster, the Executive Director of the American Association for a Democratic Germany sent a telegram to the President urging action in the form of an airlift. He wrote:

> THE PRESIDENT
> THE WHITE HOUSE
> RUSSIAN EFFORTS TO DRIVE WESTERN POWERS FROM BERLIN ARE A CRITICAL CHALLENGE TO AMERICAN FOREIGN POLICY SURRENDER WOULD DELIVER TO RUSSIAN VENGEANCE TWO MILLION GERMANS WHO HAVE DEFIED COMMUNIST TOTALITARIANISM. THERE ARE DISTURBING RUMORS OF PLANS TO EVACUATE BERLIN BECAUSE OF RUSSIAN BLOCKADE AGAINST GERMAN CIVILIAN SUPPLIES. ESSENTIAL SUPPLIES FOR THE GERMAN POPULATION CAN BE DELIVERED BY AIR AND IF NECESSARY MUST BE AT WHATEVER COST. WE URGE YOU TO MAKE THIS COUNTRY'S POSITION UNMISTAKABLE BY DECLARING THAT UNDER ALL CIRCUMSTANCES SHORT OF WAR WE WILL REMAIN IN BERLIN AND MAINTAIN SUPPLIES FOR THE CIVILIAN POPULATION. NOTHING LESS CAN ADEQUATELY REASSURE DEMOCRATIC FORCES IN GERMANY AND ELSEWHERE THAT THIS COUNTRY WILL NOT DESERT THEM.

By chance, William Draper and General Albert Wedemeyer were in Europe on a tour of inspection when the blockade began. Draper had been General Clay's economic advisor in Berlin prior to his appointment as army undersecretary. Wedemeyer had been a theatre commander whose troops were successfully supplied over the Himalayan 'hump' by General William Turner's transport aircraft. Both men quickly assessed the situation and placed their support behind the plan to supply Berlin by air. Clay still had reservations about the prospects of successfully supplying Berlin, but with no other viable alternative available, he authorised the operation.

On 26 June, Clay's decision to initiate the operation to supply Berlin by air was supported by Truman at a cabinet meeting. The President ordered the airlift to be organised as a full-scale operation using all the resources that the European Command could muster. There is no doubt that at this time the operation was being viewed on both sides of the Atlantic as a temporary measure pending the breaking of the diplomatic deadlock. However, time was of the essence. Berlin had to be supplied quickly as there were only limited stockpiles of essentials in the city. Operation Vittles was launched with approximately eighty C-47 Dakotas which flew two daily round trips into RAF Gatow and the American air base at Tempelhof. The following day, Clay sent a cable to Draper urging the expansion of the operation:

> I have already arranged for our maximum airlift to start on Monday (28 June) ... Our two Berlin airports can handle in the neighborhood of fifty additional airplanes per day. These would have to be C-47's, C-54's or planes with similar landing characteristics as our airports cannot take larger planes. LeMay is urging two C-54 groups. With this airlift, we should be able to bring in 600 or 700 tons a day. While 2,000 tons is required in normal foods, 600 tons a day (utilizing dried foods to the maximum extent) will substantially increase the morale of the German people and will unquestionably seriously disturb the Soviet blockade. To accomplish this, it is urgent that we be given approximately 50 additional transport planes to arrive in Germany at the earliest practicable date, and each day's delay will of course decrease our ability to sustain our position in Berlin Crews would be needed to permit maximum operation of these planes.

Clay got his aircraft, and soon fifty C-54 Skymasters augmented the supply effort, each one capable of delivering nine tons, three times the payload of the ageing but dependable Dakotas. On the ground, workers learned to unload the precious cargo in just seven minutes. Clay was satisfied, but still regarded the airlift as a temporary measure. On 10 July, he passed on a recommendation for armed intervention on the ground if the blockade was not lifted by a specific date. Not surprisingly, his plan to deploy infantry, tank destroyers and engineers to force open a route was rejected by Washington.

Having barely recovered from six years of total war, Great Britain was in no position to mount a sustained relief effort. Despite this, General Robertson, the British Military Governor in Germany telephoned the Headquarters of the British Air Forces of Occupation on 24 June stating emphatically that, 'Something must be done and something must be done at once'. The foreign secretary shared this view saying, 'Do your best'. These were hardly precise instructions, but nonetheless RAF Transport Command rose to the task. Following Bevin's exhortation, the British operation, codenamed Plainfare was supplemented by thirty-eight Dakotas and forty four-engine Avro Yorks (an aircraft with similar characteristics to the American C-54). In sending these additional aircraft, the British government was like the Americans, gambling on a short-term commitment.

C-47 aircraft waiting on the tarmac during the Berlin Airlift. (*Wikimedia Commons*)

Volunteers unloading flour from a C-74 aircraft during the Berlin Airlift. (*Wikimedia Commons*)

As June turned to July, the weather swiftly deteriorated. Low clouds and pelting rain turned airfields into quagmires. The Rhein-Main airfield was re-christened 'Rhein-Mud'. At Wunstorf, twenty-six Dakotas were grounded due to electrical failures. Conditions were so poor that in an interview at RAF Gatow, Group Captain Brian C. Yarde told reporters that, 'Normally planes would have stayed on the ground, but the present crisis required them to fly'. Equipment shortages served to compound the situation, with petrol bowsers, engine starter trollies and wheel chocks being in short supply. Stretched to the limit, Transport Command also encountered difficulties with refuelling and loading. While not an auspicious beginning, the operation was at least under way.

Transport Command's strength in Germany had been augmented by the arrival of the first squadron of Handley-Page Hastings at the Schleswigland airbase in November. However, five months into the airlift, there were still too few machines available for the herculean task of supplying Berlin. Officialdom then turned to the civil sector. The aviation pioneer Sir Alan Cobham supplied two Lancastrian tanker aircraft through his firm Flight Refuelling Limited. The larger civil airlines proved reluctant to divert their aircraft from lucrative commercial routes. Therefore, the authorities turned to the smaller airlines, most of whom were small-scale enterprises operating with only one or two aircraft. These operators provided valuable assistance, but the problem of aircraft numbers was still far from being solved.

Enter Freddie Laker, an aircraft dealer who owned twelve Halifax bombers that had been converted into a civil aircraft known as the Halton. With impeccable timing, he forged a deal with Bond Air Services, a company in a dire financial situation with mounting debts. Laker supplied the aircraft, while this ailing concern provided the company name. Six Haltons were sold off to provide capital, while the other six were used in the airlift. Over a period of fifty-four weeks, Laker's aircraft flew 4,700 sorties. His pilots were all former RAF veterans, some of whom had experienced the searchlights, flak, and night fighters over 'The Big City' as Bomber Harris' 'Old Lags'. During September, it must have seemed like old times as the Soviets conducted air-defence exercises.

Meanwhile, attempts went on to find a diplomatic solution. Stalin made it clear that if a West German state emerged, the presence of the Allies in Berlin would be superfluous as it would no longer be the capital. Policymakers in London and Washington concluded that Stalin's sole purpose was to prevent the creation of a democratic West Germany. Western planners remained pessimistic about the prospects of continuing the airlift beyond October.

However, in many quarters, the will to resist Soviet aggression remained strong. On 13 October, Truman received a letter from the President of the Long Beach Chamber of Commerce, C. E. Scott:

> Dear President Truman
> Our national affairs committee has given much of its attention to the present international situation. That committee urged and our Board of Directors on 11 October approved a motion placing our Chamber of Commerce on record as backing the federal government in its decision to take a strong stand in the present Berlin and German crisis.
>
> We recommend that the United States not retreat from Berlin in the face of Russian threats since such retreat would ultimately throw all of Western Europe into the Russian sphere of influence. It is also recommended that the federal government continue its present practice of using all reasonable diplomatic means possible to avoid war.

On 27 October, the President received a much more forthright appeal to action by telegram from the congressman P. E. Peden:

> THE PRESIDENT
> THE WHITE HOUSE
> NOW IS THE TIME TO ACT WITH REGARD TO REMOVING THE BERLIN BLOCKADE. THE DECISION TO SETTLE THIS DISPUTE AS VETOED BY RUSSIA IS FRESH ON THE MINDS OF THE WHOLE WORLD. THE OLD SAYING 'HE WHO HESITATES IS LOST' IS EQUALLY TRUE NOW AS IN TIME OF WAR. LET US AS A NATION LOOK THE ISSUE SQUARELY IN THE FACE AND ACT.
>
> OUR ACCEPTANCE OF THE RUSSIAN VETO TO THE UN PROPOSAL TO SETTLE THE BERLIN BLOCKADE SHOULD END BY TAKING THE NECESSARY STEPS TO MOVE SUPPLIES EITHER BY RAIL OR CONVOY INTO BERLIN. THE PEOPLE OF THIS COUNTRY WILL ENTHUSIASTICALLY RESPOND TO SUCH POSITIVE AND DETERMINED LEADERSHIP.
>
> WE ARE NOT A NATION OF COWARDS. LET US NOT HAVE RUSSIA THINK SO. THE ISSUE MUST BE MET SQUARELY WITH THE SAME DETERMINATION AND COURAGE AS HAD BY THE 300,000 WHO NOW LAY DEAD AS A RESULT OF WORLD WAR II. HAD THEY THE POWER TO DECIDE THIS ISSUE TODAY THE TRUCKS AND TRAINS WOULD ROLL ON TO BERLIN. IS IT NOT OUR DUTY TO THESE DEAD AND TO THE FUTURE OF TOMORROW THAT WE ACT 'HEART WITHIN AND GOD OVERHEAD'.

The overheated congressman was not alone in advocating more direct action. General Clay continued to push for an armoured column smashing its way through the blockade. Clay's demands continued to fall on deaf ears. Truman had already raised the stakes by stationing sixty B-29 nuclear capable bombers on British airfields. Moscow no doubt had intelligence that the bombers were not carrying nuclear weapons. However, the threat was clear. For Clay, his own version of the Charge of the Light Brigade had been superseded by the explicit threat of nuclear retaliation.

Meanwhile, inside West Berlin, electricity was only available for four hours per day. People were cold and hungry, but their spirits were kept up by the Radio in American Sector (RIAS) programme *The Islanders*. This satirical news programme featured 'typical' Berliners such as housewives, workers, teachers, and Communist functionaries. With a mixture of truth and ridicule, the programme tickled the funny bone with lines such as, 'To insure a warm Christmas, shift the date to 25 July'. The dried foods that made up a large part of peoples diet also came in for ridicule, 'Decorations for Christmas should be no problem, the Allies would fly in powdered Christmas trees that can be reconstituted with water'. Later, Clay was heard to remark that, 'Along with the airlift RIAS was one of the most important weapons in the Cold War'.

The pessimism of many military advisors and government officials proved unfounded, as by December, the airlift was bringing in 4,500 tons of supplies per day. At the Gatow and Tempelhof airfields, aircraft were touching-down every ninety seconds. A third airfield, Tegel began operations a month earlier following a remarkable feat of construction which saw the project completed in ninety days. After a wet summer, the winter turned out to be unusually mild. Enough aid was now coming into Berlin to stimulate production and by doing so, prevent an economic collapse. The gamble to supply Berlin by air was clearly paying off.

By March 1949, the airlift had not only gathered momentum, but had established a rhythm of its own. That month, aircraft delivered ninety-three per cent of their food target and exceed their coal delivery target by sixteen percent. The Kremlin must have realised by now that whatever political leverage the blockade afforded was rapidly diminishing. Added to which, the prospect of more seasonal weather rendered any possibility of the airlift failing all but non-existent. By the following month, tonnage had improved even further, with food deliveries exceeding the target by five per cent and coal deliveries by an impressive forty-nine per cent.

The success of the airlift meant that time was clearly working in the West's favour. The reverse can be said for the Soviets, as the daily spectacle of babies, children, and the elderly being deliberately starved by a callous regime served to alienate public opinion. While Stalin was not overly concerned with public opinion, he could see that the blockade was counterproductive. His failing gamble had also galvanised the West into forging the basis of an anti-Soviet military coalition backed by American economic and industrial might. It therefore made sense for Stalin to call off the blockade in May as a political defeat was preferable to a military one.

For the Allies, the airlift marked their first substantial victory in the Cold War. Berlin housewife Erika Demitrowitz recalled her feelings about the operation while attending the sixtieth anniversary commemoration of the airlift at Tempelhof Airfield in 2008:

> Our enemies who had once dropped bombs on us were now bringing us food, and coal to heat our homes with. I can remember the day the airlift was over—we picked all the flowers we could and took them to the Americans. That was our thank you.

Also present at the commemoration was the original 'Candy Bomber', Colonel Gail Halvorsen. Having initiated what came to be known as 'Operation Little Vittles' without official sanction, Halvorsen went on to become a hero to many in Berlin, his actions having a substantial impact on American–German relations for years to come. In his usual self-deprecating manner, Halvorsen remarked at the commemoration that, 'We only worked for them for a few months, and for fifty-nine years they've been spoiling us with gratitude. It's incredible'. In more recent years, there may have been foreign policy differences between America, Great Britain, and Germany, but the legacy of the airlift remains undimmed.

A C-54 aircraft dropping candy during the Berlin Airlift. (*Wikimedia Commons*)

8

Tempelhof Viewpoints

Viewpoint (B1): Hunger Fork Memorial (Platz der Luftbrücke, Berlin)

Design and symbolism

The colloquially known Hunger Fork Memorial was designed by Eduard Ludwig, a former student of Ludwig Mies van der Rohe and Walter Gropius. During the Second World War, Ludwig served in a construction unit based at Crossen An der Oder designing air raid shelters. In 1946, he became a professor at the University of Architecture and Design in Berlin. Ludwig was killed in a road traffic accident on the Berlin AVUS in 1960 while driving a red sports car at high speed.

Ludwig's plans for the airlift memorial were accepted by a panel from the West Berlin City Assembly which considered 323 other entries. The original design featured aluminium cladding. However, due to budget constraints this expensive material was substituted by stark reinforced concrete. The curved twenty-metre-high structure resembles both an outstretched hand, and a somewhat inelegant fork. In reality, the structure was meant to symbolise a broken bridge with the three prongs each representing an air corridor into Berlin. The memorial was inaugurated on 10 July 1951. The minister for All-German Affairs, Jakob Kaiser, noted the occasion by stating:

> The memorial is a symbol of a world-moving solidarity between the people of Berlin and yesterday's victors.... The airlift memorial is a memorial of the fact that Berlin has incontestably acquired the right to be the capital of our fatherland.

The Hunger Folk Memorial. (*Wikimedia Commons*)

Forty-three years later, Kaiser's prophetic words came to fruition with the withdrawal of the Allies from Berlin following the end of the Cold War. In a moving ceremony on the Platz der Luftbrücke, The British prime minister, John Major, the French president, François Mitterrand, and the American secretary of state, Warren Christopher commemorated the seventy men whose names are inscribed on the memorial.

Today, the memorial continues to symbolise the righteous struggle against the forces of totalitarianism. As such, the 'Hunger Fork' serves to enhance Tempelhof's status as a 'symbol of freedom'. More recently, the memorial was incorporated into the logo of the 'Vote Yes' campaign which sought to protect the status of the airport and prevent encroachment by developers. The campaign proved successful, and today Tempelhof has taken on a new lease of life as a publicly owned arts, and recreation space.

Viewpoint (B2): Tempelhof Airport (Platz der Luftbrücke, 5, Berlin)

Gateway to the World

Tempelhof Airport is as historically burdened as any other structure dating from the National Socialist period. However, as Claire Copley stated in her 2016 Dyos prize winning paper *Curating Tempelhof*, 'The meanings attached to places are not immutable'. Indeed, it can be seen that Tempelhof's role during the Berlin airlift has created a historical veneer which has overlaid the airport's associations with the brutal realities of Hitler's Germany. Today, Tempelhof is largely associated with the freedoms enjoyed in a democratic state, and not with the oppression and violence which characterised the Third Reich.

The airlift cemented Tempelhof's status as West Berlin's 'gateway to the world' which was an epithet hard earned. Over the period 15/16 April 1949, 1,398 aircraft touched down on Berlin's three airfields. The 12,940 tons of cargo unloaded over these two days would have taken up twenty-two trains, each pulling fifty freight cars. Tempelhof was so busy during this period that any pilot who could not land had to return to base fully loaded, there being no time to reschedule landings.

Following the lifting of the blockade, Tempelhof remained an important transport hub as it provided a means of circumventing the East German control points. Between 1963 and 1983, at least thirteen Polish Airlines (LOT) were hijacked and diverted to Tempelhof. Local wags soon christened LOT with the moniker 'Lands Often at Tempelhof'. The beginning of the end came in 1960 when the French started transferring flights to Tegel. The American airline Pan Am continued to use Tempelhof for reasons of prestige, having operated transatlantic flights from there since 1954.

In 1971, some five-and-a-half million passengers passed through the airport. However, its glory days were coming to an end. In 1975, Pan Am reluctantly transferred its operations to Tegel. The introduction of business flights and light passenger aircraft in 1985 meant that Tempelhof remained a viable proposition. However, the death knell was sounded in December 1989 when the German airlines Lufthansa and Interflug met to discuss the need for a single facility based upon the 'single airport concept'. The Berlin–Brandenburg development which developed from these discussions has turned into something of a financial and political fiasco, with the planned opening being subject to delay after delay. Meanwhile, Tempelhof has found a new lease of life, not as an airport, but as a public utility and recreational space.

Tempelhof Airport.

The Tempelhof Project run English speaking tours throughout the year. Tours are approximately of two hours duration.
Wednesday, Friday, Saturday, and Sunday (13:30 hrs)
Thursday (August and September) (13:30 hrs)
Tel. 0049 302000374-41
Web: tour@thf-berlin.de

9

The First and Last—Wilhelm Pieck

Wilhelm Pieck, the son of coachman Friedrich Pieck and his wife Auguste, was born in Guben on 3 January 1876. His mother died when he was still in early infancy. Pieck's father remarried soon afterwards to the washerwoman Wilhelmine Bahro. At school, Pieck was a serious young student, his official biographer, Walter Bartel, describing him as someone who was 'diligent and finished his schoolwork and homework punctually and properly'. He was equally conscientious during his four-year unpaid apprenticeship as a carpenter. It was while being apprenticed to his uncaring and greedy master that Pieck experienced his political awakening after joining the Wood Worker's Federation. While still apprenticed, the young trade unionist volunteered to carry the red flag at the annual May Day parade. His master warned him that if he did so, it would mean the end of his apprenticeship. Knowing the consequences, he went ahead and carried it anyway. With time on his hands, Pieck saw an opportunity to further develop his political consciousness by joining the Social Democratic Party which opposed the exploitation of the workers by their rapacious bosses. In 1899, Pieck became the chairman of the party urban district, and in 1906 took over as party secretary.

At this time, the Social Democratic Party was beset by internecine strife. Eduard Bernstein's right-wing argued that the polarisation between workers and the capitalist bosses anticipated by Marx would never materialise because of rising standards of living. The party chairman, August Bebel, remained a Marxist, but rejected the revolutionary route to power. The radical wing of the party led by Rosa Luxemburg, whose 1906 publication *The Mass Strike, the Political Party and the Trade Unions* postulated that a general strike had the power to radicalise the workers and bring about a socialist revolution. Her militant stance was evidenced in a letter to the socialist radical Clara Zetkin in which she sharply criticised the party leadership:

> The situation is simply this: August Bebel, and still more so the others, have completely spent themselves on behalf of parliamentarism and in parliamentary struggles. Whenever anything happens which transcends the limits of parliamentarism, they are completely hopeless—no, even worse than that, they try their best to force everything back into the parliamentary mould, and they will furiously attack as an enemy of the people anyone who wants to go beyond these limits.

Luxemburg was also a superb orator, whose powerful style commanded respect. Bertram D. Wolfe wrote of her magnetic stage presence:

> Physically, Rosa did not seem made to be a tragic heroine or a leader of men. A childhood hip ailment had left her body twisted, frail, and slight. She walked with an ungainly limp, but when she spoke, what people saw were large expressive eyes glowing with compassion, sparkling with laughter, burning with combativeness, flashing with irony and scorn. When she took to the floor at congress meetings, her slight frame seemed to grow taller and more commanding. Her voice was warm and vibrant, her wit deadly, her arguments wide ranging and addressed, as a rule more to the intelligence than to the feelings of her auditors.

Pieck could not fail to be impressed, and quickly fell under Luxemburg's spell. He joined the radical wing of the party which had by now also adopted the anti-militarist stance advocated by Karl Liebknecht. Pieck, along with a group of party activists, actively campaigned against Germany's participation in the First World War. In May 1915, Liebknecht published a pamphlet entitled *The Main Enemy is at Home!* Which argued that the real enemy was German imperialism, militarism, and capitalism:

> The main enemy of the German people is in Germany: German imperialism, the German war party, and German secret diplomacy. The enemy at home must be fought by the German people in a political struggle, cooperating with the proletariat of other countries whose struggle is against their own imperialists. We think as one with the German people—we have nothing in common with the German Tirpitzes and Falkenhayns, with the German government of political oppression and social enslavement. Nothing for them, everything for the German people. Everything for the international proletariat, for the sake of the German proletariat and downtrodden humanity.

The activities of the group did not go unnoticed by the authorities. Several members, including Pieck, were subsequently arrested and imprisoned. Liebknecht escaped imprisonment, as being a member of the Reichstag conferred on him parliamentary immunity.

Following their release from prison, the group founded a new underground organisation called the Spartacus League. In their illegal newspaper *Spartacus Letters,* they argued that the current nationalist conflict could be transformed into a revolutionary war. After a period of underground activity, the Spartacists came out into the open on 1 May 1916. The anti-war demonstration in Berlin's Potsdamer Platz attracted a crowd of approximately 10,000 people. An onlooker reported that, 'It was a great success. At eight o' clock in the morning a dense throng of workers assembled in the square, which the police had already occupied well ahead of time. Karl Liebknecht, in uniform, and Rosa Luxemburg were in the midst of the demonstrators and greeted with cheers from all sides'. The police waded into the demonstrators, batons flailing. Amidst violent scenes, both Liebknecht and Luxemburg were arrested. The military judicial authorities revoked Liebknecht's parliamentary immunity on 28 June, after which he was sentenced to two-and-a half-years' hard labour. Pieck fled to Amsterdam, where he lived in self-imposed exile until November 1918.

Shortly after his return to Berlin, Pieck joined the newly formed Communist Party of Germany. On 29 December, Chancellor Friedrich Ebert granted permission for the publishing of a Social Democratic Party leaflet condemning the activities of the Spartacists:

> The shameless doings of Karl Liebknecht and Rosa Luxemburg besmirch the revolution and endanger its achievements. The masses cannot afford to wait a minute longer and quietly look on while these brutes and their hangers-on cripple the activity of the republican authorities, incite the people deeper and deeper into civil war, and strangle the right of free speech with their dirty hands. With lies, slander, and violence they want to tear down everything that dares to stand in their way. With an insolence exceeding all bounds they act as though they were masters of Berlin.

Undeterred by Ebert's stinging rebuke, Liebknecht and Pieck published a leaflet calling for a national revolution. Significantly, Luxemburg was not involved in drafting the proclamation which read:

> The Ebert-Scheidemann government has become intolerable. The undersigned revolutionary committee, representing the revolutionary

> workers and soldiers, proclaims its removal. The undersigned revolutionary committee assumes provisionally the functions of government.

Luxemburg was reported to have been furious at what she regarded as an ill-conceived grab for power by a tiny fringe faction which stood little real chance of mobilising the masses on its own. Nonetheless, she reluctantly agreed to support the coming revolutionary action.

Meanwhile, Ebert had concluded a pact with the political general Wilhelm Groener. The embattled and vulnerable chancellor promised to maintain the Army if it would in turn support him in crushing the Marxist threat. Groener readily assented, as his aim was to 'win a share of power in the new state for the army and the officer corps.... To preserve the best and strongest elements of old Prussia' Ebert could also call on the services of recently raised Freikorps units whose members included former officers, elite storm troopers, adventurers, fanatical nationalists, and unemployed youths. The political stakes could not have been higher, but he was willing to use 'the armed power of the far-right to impose the government's will upon recalcitrant workers, irrespective of the long-term effects of such a policy on the stability of parliamentary democracy'. Revolutionary force was to be met with the overwhelming force of the state.

The dismissal of Berlin's chief of police by the Prussian cabinet served as the catalyst for revolutionary action. Emil Eichhorn was an Independent Social Democrat who usurped this position during the tumultuous events of 9 November 1918. He protested that the cabinet no longer had any validity, stating that, 'I got my job from the revolution, and I shall give it up only to the revolution'. Eichhorn's dismissal united shop stewards, Communists and other members of the radical left into forming a unified fighting front, determined to unseat the government by violent means.

On 30 December, elements of the revolutionary left met at the reception hall of the Berlin City Council to found the Communist Party of Germany. Gustav Noske, acting as Ebert's defence minister mobilised forces to meet this new threat. Ebert then moved his government to the safety of the town of Weimar. Meanwhile, in the capital, heavily armed troops and Friekorps units clashed with the revolutionaries who had successfully occupied several key government buildings. No quarter was given to Spartacist elements in what came to be known as 'Bloody Week'. By 8 January, several key locations, including the government printing office had been recaptured. The fragile coalition of revolutionaries began to fragment. Three days later, government forces recaptured the main revolutionary stronghold at the police headquarters building. Surveying the situation, Liebknecht made the fatalistic observation that, 'Ultimately one should accept history as it develops'.

By 13 January, the revolution was effectively over. The round-up of the Spartacist leaders began soon after. Pieck was arrested at a friend's house along with Liebknecht and Luxemburg on 15 January. They were taken to the Hotel Eden where Pieck managed to slip away as Liebknecht and Luxemburg were being questioned by Friekorps commander Waldemar Pabst. Paul Frolich, author of *Rosa Luxemburg: Her Life and Work* described what happened next:

> A short while after Liebknecht had been taken away to be executed, Rosa Luxemburg was led out of the hotel by First Lieutenant Vogel. Awaiting her was Runge, who had received an order from Vogel and Pflugk-Hartung to strike her to the ground. With two blows of a rifle butt, her skull was smashed. Her almost lifeless body was flung into a waiting car, and several officers jumped in. One of them struck Rosa on the head with the butt of a revolver, and Vogel finished her off with a shot to the head. Her corpse was then driven to the Tiergarten and, on Vogel's orders, thrown from the Liechtenstein Bridge into the Landwehr Canal, where it was not washed up until 31 May.

Within months of the crushing of the Spartacist revolution, the radical left split into two factions following the founding of the Communist Workers Party of Germany. In November, the government initiated a state sponsored purge of Spartacist elements. Pieck left for exile in Italy.

Following his return to Germany in 1921, Pieck became an active member the Communist Party of Germany, which under the leadership of Paul Levi had greatly increased its membership, becoming a mass party for the first time. In 1922, Pieck became a founding member of International Red Aid, an organisation established by the Communist International to provide material and moral aid to prisoners of the 'class war'. He also wrote articles for the party newspaper *The Red Flag*. In 1924, Pieck attended Lenin's funeral in Moscow. A diary entry from 23 January 1924 reads:

> The earth is covered with a thick layer of snow. It is a cold and bright winter day. Lenin lies in the room. His face is a pale yellow, but the skin is smooth—there is practically not a wrinkle left. How hard it is to become reconciled to the thought that he is no longer! Silent, with tears in their eyes, veterans of the Civil War carry him out of the room. The mournful bearers, carrying the dead leader, wend their way along a narrow path across an open snow-covered field to the railway station. Crowds of people—old and young—have assembled near the station. The heart-warming strains of the funeral march float in the air.

> Moscow. Hundreds and thousands of people line the streets. An endless procession is moving to the House of Trade Unions where Lenin lies in his bier. Old Bolsheviks—Lenin's closest friends and associates—stand in the first guard of honour. Comrade Stalin and other members of the Political Bureau are among them. Comrade Krupakaya stands by the side of her dead husband.
>
> It is bitterly cold outside. Thirty degrees and more below zero. Day and night masses of people flock to the centre of the city. They stand in the street for hours on end. Bonfires are burning. And in endless lines the people march past the bier holding the remains of the dead Lenin. For four days and four nights they never stop marching. It is something unsurpassed and awe-inspiring!

Pieck served as an elected member of the Prussian parliament between 1921 and 1928. He then served as a Reichstag deputy until Hitler's ascent to power in 1933 forced him into exile, first in Prague, then Paris. In 1936, Pieck relocated to Moscow, from where he became a vocal critic of the excesses of Hitler's regime.

Following the German defeat at Stalingrad, Pieck helped to found the National Committee for a Free Germany. This was a Moscow-based group made up of exiled German Communists and re-educated German prisoners of war. On 12 July 1943, thirty-eight members of the Committee signed a manifesto urging the German public and Wehrmacht to fight against Hitler, and in doing so support the democratic, socialist revival of Germany. Prussians who had allied themselves with Russia against Napoleon were portrayed as exemplars, serving to stimulate the spirit of resistance against Hitler's regime:

> We have a great role model in our history. A hundred and thirty years ago, when German troops were still on Russian ground as enemies, the best Germans, von Stein, Arndt, Clausewitz, Yorck, and others, sent an address from Russia to the conscience of the German people, above the heads of the traitorous authorities, and called upon the nation to fight for freedom. Like them, we will stake all of our strength and our lives to undertake everything that benefits our nation's struggle for freedom and the acceleration of Hitler's fall.

The signing of the manifesto was meant to stimulate the growth of similar groups across the globe. However, as Georgy Dimitrov (general secretary of the Communist International) noted in his diary in August 1943, the development of groups along similar lines in Hungary, Romania and Italy was abandoned due to 'unfavourable discussions in England and America regarding the German Free Germany Committee'. Indeed, some political analysts in the West believed that the main aim of the Committee was to secure a separate peace with Germany. In reality, the Kremlin envisaged this group of exiles and former prisoners taking on a wide range of roles, including the overthrow of the Hitler regime, saving Germany from complete destruction, and the establishment of a democratic socialist republic. However, the failed attempt on Hitler's life in July 1944 meant that the power of the German military aristocracy was broken for good, and with it, any real chance of a revolution within Germany. Henceforth, interest in the Committee waned. Nonetheless, it was destined to play a role in the Soviet occupation of Germany.

From the autumn of 1944 onwards, the leadership of the Committee, particularly Ulbricht and Pieck, directed the energy of group members towards the post-war occupation of Germany. Their tasks included, supervising the propaganda aimed at Wehrmacht personnel in Soviet captivity, training operatives and identifying suitable people for appointments in the post-war administration, and forming work commissions and task forces to prepare for German reconstruction. In the last stages of the war, some exiles returned to assist Soviet commanders administer German territories occupied by the Red Army.

On 30 April 1945, the exiled German Communists, led by Ulbricht and Pieck returned to Germany. Their immediate task was to begin building local administrations in Berlin's twenty districts. In each district they sought out Social Democrats and qualified civil servants willing to work with the Soviet authorities. Dedicated Communists were to be installed in each district to oversee administration and personnel departments. According to Pieck, the overall aim of the group was to 'complete the civil-democratic revolution through a civil-democratic government'.

On 11 June 1945, the Central Committee of the German Communist Party issued a proclamation which promised the establishment of an anti-fascist democratic republic with rights and freedoms for all. The proclamation read:

> Working people in the City and Countryside!
> Men and Women!
> German Youth!
> Wherever we look, we see ruins, rubble and ashes. Our cities are destroyed, immense, once-fertile regions are desolate and deserted. The economy is in a shambles and utterly paralysed. Millions upon millions of people have been devoured by a war that was caused by the Hitler regime. Millions have been cast into extreme hardship and abject misery. A catastrophe of unimaginable proportions has befallen Germany, and

the spectre of homelessness, pestilence, unemployment, and hunger peers out at us from the ruins....

The Hitler regime has proved the ruin of Germany, for with its policy of aggression and violence, plundering, war, and genocide, Hitler has brought destruction unto our people and has burdened them with heavy guilt and responsibility in the eyes of the civilised world....

Fortunately, the cause of justice, freedom, and progress stood on the side of the United Nations, with the Soviet Union, England, and America at the head. Through their sacrifices, the Red Army and the armies of the Allies saved the cause of humanity from Hitler's barbarism. They shattered Hitler's armies, demolished Hitler's state, and thereby also led you, the working German population, out of the chains of Hitler's slavery and into peace and liberation.

Today, at the end of the Third Reich, after all the suffering and misfortune, all the shame and disgrace, after the darkest era in German history, the Social Democratic German worker will agree with us that the fascist plague was only able to spread through Germany because in 1918 those who were responsible for the war, and those who had committed war crimes went unpunished, because the struggle for a genuine democracy was not waged, because the Weimar Republic gave free rein to reactionary forces, because the anti-Soviet agitation of a few democratic leaders paved the way for Hitler, and because the rejection of a unified anti-fascist front paralysed the people....

The German Communist Party was and is the party of the resolute struggle against militarism, imperialism, and imperialistic wars. The party has never deviated from this path. The party has always kept pure the banner of Karl Liebknecht and Rosa Luxemburg, Ernst Thalmann, and Jonny Schehr. We Communists look back with pride on these struggles, which claimed the lives of our best and most faithful comrades. We warned early and insistently against the imperialistic path, warned that Hitler would inevitably lead Germany into catastrophe....

The task now is to learn the lessons of the past, thoroughly and forever. We must break completely new ground! Every German must become aware that the path our people took previously was a false path.... May the rebuilding of Germany take place on a solid foundation.... With the destruction of Hitlerism it is also important to complete the democratisation of Germany.... We are of the opinion that forcing the Soviet system onto Germany would be the false path, for this path does not suit the present conditions of German development. Rather, we are of the opinion that the most compelling interests of the German people in the present situation call for Germany to take a different path, the path of establishing an anti-fascist, democratic regime, a parliamentary,

> democratic republic with all the democratic rights and liberties for the people. At this present historic transition, we Communists call for all working people, for all democratic and progressive forces to join together to fight for the democratic renewal of Germany, for the rebirth of our country ...
>
> A new page has been turned in the history of the German people. New insights are forcing their way forward from the lessons of Germany's collapse.
>
> We declare: firm unity, a resolute struggle, and a determined effort to guarantee that our cause will be successful! Let us march forward, holding our heads high! Let us begin the task with all our strength. For then, out of destitution and death, out of ruins and disgrace, freedom for our people and a new life of dignity will arise!

The democratic worker's utopia promised in the proclamation never materialised. The party leadership had their own vision of post-war German politics which did not include democratic freedoms. This vision was articulated by Ulbricht who said, 'It must look democratic but we must control everything'.

Many Germans had good reason to be wary of the 'sudden affinity for democracy' shown by the Communists. The public remained unaware that the softening of their image came about following the expression of concerns in Moscow and Berlin that a radical revolutionary path would never secure a broad base of support for the party. Pieck was wary of this new approach, arguing that German unity depended upon Communist dominance of the political arena throughout Germany. Such dominance proved an illusion. Nonetheless, it suited Ulbricht's book as it enabled him to wholly concentrate on consolidating power both within the party and in the Soviet occupation zone.

On 7 October 1949, the Soviets and German Communists relaunched the occupied zone as the German Democratic Republic. Article three of the constitution propagated the myth of democracy:

> All state authority emanates from the people. Every citizen has the right and the duty to take part in the formation of political life in the community, county, state, and the German Democratic Republic. State authority must serve the welfare of the people, liberty, peace, and the progress of democracy. Those active in public service are servants of the community as a whole and are not part of any one party. Their activity is supervised by the popular representative body.

Following his election as president, Pieck perpetuated the myth of democracy. He stated in his inaugural address that, 'We stand today at the turning point of German history'. However, to assure the dialectical process alluded to by Pieck, the state's past, present, and future needed restructuring in order to fit into the Communist conception of progress. This restructuring would in time lead to economic and social disaster as the dialectical tools to deal with changing markets and changing social mores simply did not exist.

Against a background of social discord and economic collapse, Pieck's health deteriorated. Having already suffered one stroke, he had a second major episode in July 1953. At the time he was also diagnosed with progressive cirrhosis of the liver. As most executive authority already lay in Ulbricht's hands, Pieck became no more than a figurehead. In August 1960, he retired to a new summer residence close to the ruins of Hermann Göring's 'Carinhall'. A month later, Pieck died of heart failure, aged eighty-four. Following his death, Ulbricht introduced an executive committee which replaced the office of president. Pieck therefore holds the dubious distinction of being the first and last president of the German Democratic Republic.

A 1972-dated DDR coin bearing the image of Wilhelm Pieck. (*Wikimedia Commons*)

10

'We are all of Berlin'

The political capital accrued by the West following the successful Berlin airlift did not last long. At exactly 07:00 hrs, on 29 August 1949, a team of scientists successfully detonated the first Soviet nuclear bomb near the scientific settlement at Semipalatinsk. The operation, codenamed 'Lightning' benefited greatly from intelligence acquired from the Manhattan Project which was passed on by the British physicist Klaus Fuchs, the American physicist Ted Hall, the machinist David Greenglass, the engineer Julius Rosenberg, and his wife Ethel. After his arrest, Fuchs claimed that the material which he passed on accelerated the Soviet programme 'by one year at least'. The Americans were dumbfounded. Stalin was more than satisfied. The balance had been restored.

On 5 August 1950, Stalin retired to his Abkhazian dacha on the Black Sea coast. Here, the weary titan pulled the strings in Korea, while at the same time unleashing a pogrom against alleged members of 'anti-Soviet Jewish nationalistic sabotage groups'. The Jews were not Stalin's only target, as he called for ever greater vigilance against 'the enemies within'. The camps were filled with those whose forced confessions had revealed a conspiracy to topple Stalin.

The last few years of Stalin's life were characterised by his increasing paranoia. Washington's resolute stance in Korea fuelled his apocalyptic visions, and above all his loathing of foreign influence in Soviet affairs. 'Cosmopolitanism's a widespread phenomenon' replied Stalin in response to a question from his son in law Yuri Andreyevich Zhdanov about whether the recent pogrom had focused too much on the Jews. During the Great Purge (1937–1941) many party comrades were tarred with the Trotskyist brush. Now, Stalin was happy to tar some of his closest associates including Abakumov and Molotov with the Zionist brush.

Stalin had once declaimed to his oligarchs, 'You've grown old! I'll replace you all.' Now, the Politburo heavyweights knew that he was not joking, no one was safe.

Stalin's death on 5 March 1953 effectively brought the latest round of terror to an end. Beria, the loathsome and depraved security and police chief was more relieved than anyone, as he knew that his former boss had been busy plotting his downfall. Without waiting for Stalin's body to grow cold, Beria initiated moves to liberalise the Soviet regime. In early May, the ruling triumvirate of Beria, Malenkov and Molotov summoned the hard-line Stalinist leader of East Germany to Moscow in order to discuss the implementation of liberalisation there too. Ulbricht bridled at this apparent abandonment of Marxist doctrine. During the previous summer, he had launched a crash programme dubbed 'The accelerated construction of socialism'. This Stalinist programme aimed at building a strict command economy through huge investments in heavy industry, the strangulation of private enterprise, the collectivisation of agriculture, travel restrictions and the promotion of state atheism. Predictably, the experiment was a disaster. By the time of Stalin's death, there were shortages in consumer goods, a huge budget deficit and mass migration of skilled workers to the West. Yet, despite all the evidence of failure, Ulbricht could not be persuaded to change his course.

On 14 May, the plenum of the central committee of the Socialist Unity Party moved forward on a planned purge of party members, removing Fritz Dahlem, a firm critic of Ulbricht from the Politburo. More significantly, the plenum promulgated an increase in work norms without financial compensation, thus effectively lowering wages by ten per cent. However, the new leaders in the Kremlin were determined to push for change in order to stabilise the East German economy and to convince the West of their more conciliatory attitude towards foreign policy. The East German leadership was summoned to Moscow in early June to receive instructions stemming from decisions made at the Presidium of the Soviet Communist Party on 27 May. Having been instructed to release their grip, the Berlin Communists convened in Berlin on 9 June to discuss how to implement Soviet policy. In a communique published in *Neues Deutschland* on 11 June, the regime was criticised for having made mistakes. Furthermore, a New Course was announced, reversing Ulbricht's Stalinisation programme. It looked to many that socialism was indeed losing its grip.

Alas, the New Course did not proceed as the Kremlin would have hoped. The liberalisation process did not extend to the increase in work norms. Confusion reigned as Ulbricht failed to make any attempt to gain party support. Neither did he authorise a propaganda campaign in the press to inform both party and people why this radical change in direction had been deemed necessary. Rather than calming the situation, Ulbricht had lit the blue touch paper.

On 16 June 1953, construction workers from the prestigious 'Workers' Palaces' project on Stalinallee, along with those from the building site at Friedrichshain Hospital put down their tools and marched in protest to the House of Ministries situated at the corner of Wilhelm Straße and Leipziger Straße. As the group made its way through the city, more and more people joined them, until more than 4,000 discontented workers arrived at their destination to demand an audience with the party chairman and prime minister. Both Ulbricht and Grotewohl declined the invitation. Instead, the minister of mines, Fritz Selbmann attempted to address the demonstrators. P. Naumov, the *Pravda* correspondent in Berlin witnessed the scene:

> We reached the column of striking workers at the square in front of the House of Ministries of the German Democratic Republic on Leipziger Straße. They stood in front of the building, whistling, screaming and yelling: 'We want to see Ulbricht or Grotewohl'. At the centre, one could recognise a blue cloth poster with the writing 'We demand the reduction of norms'. According to our rough estimates, the nucleus of the crowd was comprised of some 2,000 people. As many as that were standing around. Most of them were officials of the ministries who had come out onto the street out of curiosity or with the intention of talking with the workers. In a window on the first floor, Deputy Prime Minister Heinrich Rau and Minister Fritz Selbmann appeared. The latter stood by the window ledge and attempted to speak. The roar of the crowd drowned out his words. Later a small table was brought out of the building into the middle of the throng. Selbmann climbed on top of it. His very first words were booed.

Braving the crowd, Selbmann at last made his words heard. However, as the following dialogue demonstrates, he was continually challenged:

> Selbmann: Dear colleagues
> Unknown worker: You're not our colleague, you're a shit and a traitor.
> Selbmann: I voted against the increase in production norms at the 28 May session of the Council of Ministers. The increase has not been introduced in my department. I will insist that the government revoke the measures which were incorrectly adopted at the session. Go back to work calmly, and put your trust in me.
> Unknown worker: We no longer have confidence in you. We want guarantees.
> Selbmann: But I have myself been a worker for a long time.

> Unknown worker: You have forgotten that you are no longer our comrade.... We are the real Communists, not you.

Selbmann was left speechless. Then, a stonemason knocked the dumbstruck politician off the table on which he was standing with a single blow of his hand and mounted it himself. Addressing Selbmann and the demonstrators, the stonemason emphatically stated that, 'We're not in the least interested in what you have to say. We no longer wish to be your slaves. We're opposed to the work norms, and we don't all come from Stalinallee. We are all of Berlin'. Naumov, noted in his report:

> From this man we heard the demands of the strikers for the very first time: annulment of the increased work norms; decrease in prices in the state-owned businesses; a general increase in living standards for workers; abandonment of the formation of a People's Army in the Republic; holding of free elections in Germany—during this speech Selbmann came down.

The stonemason ended his superbly forceful piece of oratory by stating that Selbmann's attitude demonstrated that he was out of touch with the workers and as such was in no position to understand their demands. He went on to call for a general strike if Ulbricht and Grotewohl refused to talk to them about their just demands.

The demonstrators moved on, and for several more hours their demands and calls for a general strike could be heard echoing in the streets. Naumov, and a reporter from *Komsomolskaya Pravda* followed the demonstrators, making mental notes of their demands as they went along. Later, the two reporters wrote down the slogans repeated by the demonstrating workers:

> We demand a rise in living standards!
> We demand a reduction in work norms!
> We are workers, not slaves!
> We want to be free men!
> We demand free elections!
> We want butter, not the People's Army!
> Down with the People's Army!
> The Trading Organisation hits us with a knockout punch!
> We demand a forty per cent drop in prices at the Trading Organisation.

Naumov noted that none of the above slogans were specifically directed against the government, the party organisation, or the Soviet Union. That would come later. Meanwhile, government cars equipped with loudspeakers toured the streets in order to announce the government's decision to annul the increase in work norms. However, by now, the demonstration had developed a momentum of its own.

As the atmosphere became tenser, anyone wearing a Free German Youth shirt was liable to be beaten. The loudspeaker cars were also targeted. On Rosenthaler Platz, demonstrators dragged the driver and co-driver out and requisitioned the vehicle which for the rest of the day advertised the coming general strike. This call to arms proved very effective as even workers repairing the headquarters of the Social Unity Party downed tools and joined the demonstrators. One unnamed demonstrator later recalled:

> When I went home on the night of 16 June, I had but a single thought, I hope I'll be strong enough tomorrow and I hope everyone will be part of the movement. During the night of 16/17 June it became clear that we had to fight no matter what the consequences, and that we had to fight until the end. 16 June had transformed us all.

That evening, radio transmissions from the American sector in West Berlin made public the demands of the demonstrators and reported that there would be a general strike the following day. Meanwhile, the government held an extraordinary session of the party *Aktiv* in the Friedrichstadtpalast. Ulbricht, Grotewohl, and several other senior party officials spoke, but none directly touched on the demonstrations, nor did they give any indications as to how the government would react to the unfolding situation. Later that evening Ulbricht, Grotewohl, Politburo member Rudolf Hernstadt, Minister of State Security Wilhelm Zaisser, and the Soviet Chief Commissar Vladimir Semyenov met to discuss quelling the anticipated general strike by deploying Soviet troops in East Berlin.

Demonstrators started gathering on Stalinallee early in the morning of 17 June. More than 7,000 formed a marching column. By 09:00 hrs, this column had united with other marchers on the Unter den Linden to form a 30,000 strong cohort. Meanwhile, two more large columns were marching towards Potsdamer Platz and Alexanderplatz. Within a few hours, the whole character of the demonstration changed from that of a worker's protest to a full-blown revolution which aimed at nothing less than toppling the government. Naumov watched as the uprising gathered momentum. Although his reporting at the time had a distinct Soviet bias, it is still worth quoting *in extensio*:

> The demonstrations bore a purely political character from the beginning. Alongside the slogans from the previous day, new ones appeared 'Down with the Grotewohl government', 'down with the SED regime'. The

Walter Ulbricht. (*Wikimedia Commons*)

people dressed completely differently from the day before. No work attire could be seen. The provocateurs from West Berlin were easily recognisable by their appearance and behaviour. They were adequately represented in every column of marchers and formed the nucleus of the riot's heroes and shouters. One must say that with every stride and pace, good organisation was noticeable.

When the first processions of demonstrators marched past the USSR diplomatic mission to the GDR, many people tried to shout, to whistle, and utter insults. Momentarily men (obviously specially selected and instructed) jumped forward, calling on them not to make any noise, 'so as not to provoke the Russians'. Strike sentries were posted on the corner of the streets, and when someone or other wanted to leave the crowd of people, they pushed them back in.

The Soviet troops appeared on the streets of Berlin in the early morning. First they drove around without impeding the movement of the columns. At first they were greeted by the demonstrators with whistling and roaring, and as the atmosphere grew tenser, the insults began. I heard several times 'Russian swine' and 'ape'. Such insults could not only be heard from the ranks of the demonstrators, but also from the residents who were afraid to join the columns. It was said that in a few cases the demonstrators fell upon the cars of Soviet soldiers, even upon tanks. Sometimes they threw stones at the soldiers.

Once our car got into the middle of the crowd of people (it was still morning, their passions had not been inflamed yet). When they saw the Soviet Licence plate, some youths came towards us and shouted, threatening, 'Russians get out!' We got out of our car and mingled with the people. They did nothing to the car. Two hours after this, bandits at Alexanderplatz tipped over the car of the representative of the 'Sovexportfilm', Comrade Pronin, with him in it. At the height of the events, we came to Potsdamer Platz. A rally was being held. A stage stood in the middle. They brought a microphone and loudspeaker from the British sector. It was impossible to recognise who spoke, but the message was the same as in the RIAS broadcasts.

Then the crowd of people rushed to the 'Kolumbushaus' were there used to be a department store of the Trading Organisation. One of the People's Police officers who had been guarding the store was pushed to the side.... Soon afterwards the building was set on fire. The kiosks and billboards were likewise on fire. Around the same time, a fight broke out between a cordon of People's Police officers, who were guarding the House of the GDR Ministries on Leipziger Straße, and the putschists. The police were using their truncheons. They were almost overwhelmed, when suddenly Soviet tanks arrived and deterred the mob. Rowdies did, however, destroy the windows on the first floor.

Many riots ensued, in particular at Alexanderplatz and near the Police Headquarters. There, cars were tipped over and set on fire. The windows in the Soviet shop, 'Das Internationale Buch', were smashed. On the first floor of the Police Headquarters, not one window remained intact. In front of this very building, three police cruisers were incinerated. The People's Police did not shoot.

I myself saw cars with West German licence plates, with American and other plates, which drove around the areas where the riots took place. The demonstrators did not stop them, but sometimes greeted them enthusiastically. Besides Potsdamer Platz, there was another loudspeaker from West Berlin behind the Brandenburg Gate. Through it commands were constantly given....

Naumov paints a lurid picture of mob violence orchestrated by agent provocateurs serving western imperialist interests. His reporting reflected the blinkered thinking which dominated both East German government circles and their Soviet overlords. This was no Berlin mob, but a revolutionary movement which had spread throughout East Germany.

It is estimated that over a million people took part in nationwide protests on 17 June. The Soviet authorities seriously misjudged the strength of Ulbricht's regime. Despondent and clearly anticipating defeat, Ulbricht had retreated to the safety of the Soviet Headquarters in Berlin–Karlshorst. The situation was indeed serious, and confronted with the failure of the People's Police to quell the uprising, martial law was declared at 13:00 hrs. In a radio-telegram to Molotov and Bulganin, Semyonov describes the crushing of demonstrations throughout East Germany by Soviet armoured forces:

> We report on the situation in Berlin and the GDR at 14:00 hrs. Berlin time.
>
> The office building of the GDR government (House of Ministries), which was attacked by demonstrators, has been liberated after the arrival of tanks. The demonstrators were also repulsed from the SED Central Committee building and the Police Presidium building. The German police and our troops opened fire on the demonstrators at the Police Presidium building. We do not have information on dead and wounded.
>
> In the districts of Alexanderplatz and Pankow, demonstrators built barriers and roadblocks. The provocateurs organised a pogrom of the bookstore 'The International Book'. In some government buildings and shops, windows were smashed.
>
> Until our troops took active measures to settle the unrest, the demonstrators succeeded in overcoming resistance by the German People's Police and Garrisoned People's Police, who in general did not hold them off. With the start of active intervention by our troops, the situation in Berlin began to normalise. Demonstrators dispersed after the appearance of Soviet tanks.
>
> At 12:00 hrs. U-Bahn and S-Bahn traffic stopped as per our instruction in order to impede the arrival of provocateurs from West Berlin.
>
> At 13:00 hrs. martial law was declared in Berlin.
>
> In the past hours one can see in Berlin a certain decline in disturbances. Various worker groups have left the demonstrations and gone back to work or home.
>
> The situation in the GDR is gradually becoming normal again.
>
> The most serious situation is in the city of Gorlitz on the German-Polish border where a mob of 30,000 destroyed SED offices, the prison, and the buildings of the security service and district committee. A reinforced armour battalion with tanks was deployed to Gorlitz.
>
> In Magdeburg, provocateurs set the SED Municipal Committee building and the prison on fire and had a shootout with GDR State Security troops. Soviet troops were deployed to the city. Disturbances reached a significant scale in Halle. Some 1,000 workers from the Leuna and Buna factories, most of whom were intoxicated, overwhelmed the police protection in the factories.

> In Berlin some seventy people were arrested.
> Soviet troops operating in the GDR and troops of the People's Police detachments were given the order to use their weapons if necessary to arrest and punish the instigators of the unrest.
> We will report with further developments.

Ulbricht's survival was due solely to Soviet military intervention. He and the party leadership had become totally out of touch with the mood of the workers. Furthermore, he had failed to understand the nature of the uprising. It was too spontaneous to be a determined grab for power. Instead it took the form of a 'symbolic liberation', one characterised by the ripping down of propaganda posters, the overturning of cars, attacks on party representatives and the attempted storming of government buildings. Such actions certainly shook the nerves of the party leadership, but their effects were more apparent than real. The sinews that held together the apparatus of state control were largely unaffected.

Berthold Brecht's poem *The Solution* summed up the scale of the response to the uprising. This satirical barb aimed at Ulbricht's regime was published in the West German newspaper *Die Welt* in 1959:

> After the uprising of 17 June
> The Secretary of the Writer's Union
> Had leaflets distributed in the Stalinallee
> Stating that the people
> Had forfeited the confidence of the government
> And could win it back only
> By redoubled efforts
> Would it not be easier in that case
> For the Politburo to dissolve the people
> And elect another

The violent and repressive measures which had crushed the uprising at an estimated cost of 500 lives kept Ulbricht in power, paradoxically at a time when his rigid Stalinist methods were no longer favoured in Moscow. Rather than jettison their puppet at a time of uncertainty, the Kremlin leadership continued to support him. For the East German people, this spelled disaster.

11

Better than War

In Washington, the June uprising was not considered a significant historical event. Perhaps, this is because the intelligence services were a little slow in realising the scale of economic and political discontent within East Germany. As the revolt spread, some government hawks realised that this was more than a strike action and called for the arming of the workers. President Eisenhower knew that the uprising was a brave but doomed enterprise, and that arming the workers would 'create a situation in which they think their empire is threatened and cause actual, direct conflict between the two sides'. Eisenhower's special assistant, psychological warfare expert, General Charles Douglas Jackson saw scope for action of another kind, stating, 'Oh, this is a wonderful opportunity; we'll just exploit this to the fullest'. The indirect methods employed to exploit the propaganda opportunities thrown up by the uprising included a food-relief programme, information activities such as the successful 'Atoms for Peace' exhibit, scholarship funds enabling East Berlin students to attend the Free University of Berlin, and active encouragement with regard to the commemoration of the June uprising.

The British government appeared paralysed by indecision, as open support for the uprising would have risked damaging the fragile status quo. Indeed, the British authorities in Berlin went out of their way to discourage workers from joining the uprising. One senior officer was heard to comment, 'I've spoken to the police president in order to effect an end to the incitement, stressing in particular the distribution of leaflets via balloons'. Churchill downplayed the violent suppression of the uprising by stating that, 'I had the impression that in the light of the increasing unrest they acted with considerable restraint'. Britain's lack of support remains a sore point for Hubertus Knabe, Director of Berlin's Stasi Museum. In an interview with *The Telegraph* in June 2003, Knabe expounded his forthright views:

> The Western policy towards the protests was shameful. For years politicians in the West preached about liberating the East and encouraged easterners to stand up against Communism. But the moment hundreds and thousands went on to the streets, they turned their backs on them.

Perhaps, Knabe had a point. By allowing the uprising to fail, the West played a part in creating the conditions for an intensification of repressive measures by the bruised, but all-too-intact Communist regime.

Predictably, Ulbricht's response to the uprising and its aftermath was to tighten his grip. The authorities cut off rail and bus links into West Berlin, effectively bringing the American food-aid programme to an end, just as the winter was setting in. The round-up of strike leaders and prominent protestors had already begun. On 15 July, S. Kruglov (minister of internal affairs) sent a top-secret dispatch to Moscow outlining the process and progress of investigations into the uprising's ringleaders:

> In the investigating process of the Ministry for State Security of the German Democratic Republic there are group files on the persons who took part in the preparation and realisation of the provocation of 17 June of this year in Berlin and other cities.
>
> The investigation has established that the provocative work was carried out according to assignments given by reactionary and espionage organisations in West Germany. The most characteristic are the following files:
>
> An investigative file on seven residents of the city of Berlin. HERTEL, eighteen years old, lubricator in a transport association, MULLER, twenty-six years old, the owner of a truck, DIBALL, twenty years old, without definite occupation, and others, who took action in the riots (broke glass in government buildings and shops, tore down slogans and placards, and threw stones at the police).
>
> The arrested HERTEL and DIBBAL admitted that they took part in the riots on the instructions of the fascist organisation 'League of German Youth' of which they had been members since 1952.
>
> The arrested MULLER stated that he was drawn into participation by the representatives of the anti-Soviet organisation of West Berlin 'Fighting Group Against Inhumanity'.
>
> The file of the investigation is complete.

Ulbricht blamed his Stasi chief for not detecting or arresting the 'unreformed fascists' whom he regarded as being responsible for the

June uprising. The state-controlled press unleashed a constant barrage of anti-western invective focusing on the alleged *agent provocateurs* who were bent on causing disruption to the everyday life of citizens in the worker's paradise. These barbs served to explain the reasons behind the failing economy. Meanwhile, the real causes remained concealed, as the government simply could not admit to their failings.

The spectre of economic collapse, followed by the creation of a unified, capitalist Germany loomed large. This led Soviet policymakers and hard-liners in the East German government to decisively throw in their lot with Ulbricht. The liberalisation policies advocated by Beria were swiftly overturned. The course was now set on a hard-line policy based on greater levels of consumer austerity and increased repression. However, both Ulbricht and his Kremlin backers remained blissfully unaware of the economic miracle taking place in West Germany. More than anywhere, Berlin characterised the growing economic gap, as in this tale of two cities, one was affluent, while the other was increasingly impoverished.

The bright lights of the Kurfürstendamm in West Berlin's fashionable shopping district served as a beacon to the thousands of workers from the East who yearned for a better life. In 1953, some 300,000 East Germans fled to the West, many of them taking advantage of the easy access through the four zones of occupation which Berlin offered. Those fleeing were mostly young, well educated, and highly skilled. The Soviet Ambassador to East Germany, Mikhail Pervakhin observed:

> The presence in Berlin of an open and essentially uncontrolled border between the socialist and capitalist worlds unwittingly prompts the population to make a comparison between both parts of the city, which unfortunately, does not always turn out in favour of the Democratic East Berlin.

The booming West German economy was crying out for labour, these eager workers from industry, construction, agriculture, schools, hospitals and a host of other professions were more than willing to do their bit. In 1955, an East German propaganda campaign aimed to stop the haemorrhage of skilled workers. One leaflet dramatically described the consequences of fleeing the republic:

> Both from the moral standpoint as well as in terms of the interests of the whole German nation, leaving the Democratic Republic of Germany is an act of political and moral backwardness and depravity.
>
> Those who let themselves be recruited objectively serve West German reaction and militarism, whether they know it or not. Is it not despicable when for the sake of a few alluring job offers or the false promises about

> a 'guaranteed future' one leaves a country in which the seed for a new and more beautiful life is sprouting, and is already showing the first fruits, for the place that favours war and destruction?
>
> Is it not an act of political depravity when citizens, whether young people, workers, or members of the intelligentsia leave and betray what our people have created through common labour in our republic to offer themselves to the American and British secret services or work for the West German factory owners, Junkers, or militarists? Does not leaving the land of progress for the morass of a historically outdated social order demonstrate political backwardness and blindness?
>
> Workers throughout Germany will demand punishment for those who today leave the republic, the strong bastion of the fight for peace, to serve the deadly enemies of the German people, the imperialists and industrialists.

The propaganda campaign had no noticeable effect. Therefore, on 11 December 1957, a new passport law came into place which reduced the overall number of those fleeing to the West. Fleeing the republic became a criminal offence, carrying a prison sentence.

By circumstance, rather than design, the porous quadripartite borders in Berlin became the focal point for those planning their escape. The state-controlled press and propaganda machine continued to paint a vivid picture of women being sold into prostitution, and men toiling away in Dickensian surroundings; those that remained behind faced even tighter economic restrictions. Moreover, they were prompted to work even harder to compensate for the serious labour shortages which threatened to destroy the fragile economy. The so-called 'brain-drain' prompted the East German government to reflect on the causes of the catastrophe. In early 1961, Ulbricht told the Politburo that over sixty per cent were fleeing the republic 'due to mainly economic reasons associated with shortcomings in the workplace'. All this navel-gazing led nowhere, as Ulbricht was unwilling to waver from his Stalinist principles.

With his regime heading for a crisis that threatened its very existence, Ulbricht acted decisively. At a meeting of Warsaw Pact leaders in March 1961, he advocated erecting a barbed wire barrier to supplement the tightened border controls between East and West Berlin. Khrushchev baulked at the idea, stating that 'a total sealing off' was not part of 'current Soviet tactics'. Ulbricht did not give up, and over the following months, continued to press Khrushchev to demand a peace treaty which would render Berlin 'strictly neutral', thereby greatly restricting access to the city by the western powers. Ulbricht's persistence paid off, as Khrushchev decided to put the squeeze on Berlin once more.

Nikita Khrushchev. (*Wikimedia Commons*)

Khrushchev's opportunity to raise the temperature came in early June, when a summit meeting with President John F. Kennedy was held in Vienna. The summit turned into a pugilistic encounter as the inexperienced American president was berated on a number of issues, including 'wars of national liberation', and nuclear weapons. The atmosphere got increasingly heated as both participants threatened to start a full-scale war. Khrushchev's underestimation of Kennedy's resolve was demonstrated by his statement, 'I would like peace, but if you want war, then that's your business'. Afterwards, the bruised and battered President told *Time* magazine's White House correspondent Hugh Sidney that, 'I have never met a man like this. I talked about how a nuclear exchange would kill seventy million people in ten minutes, and he just looked at me as if to say, 'so what?' However, despite the aggressive tone which characterised the summit, it could be argued that it served some purpose.

Both leaders had looked into the nuclear abyss, neither liked what they saw. Khrushchev had said, 'Only a madman would start a war over Berlin'. Now he applied that reasoning to himself as he reluctantly acceded to Ulbricht's demand for a permanent barrier to separate East and West Berlin. Perhaps the idea of a wall was a blessing in disguise as it would serve to lower tensions and relegate Berlin's status as the number one Cold War hotspot.

Workers demarcating East and West Berlin.

Shortly after midnight on Sunday, 13 August, East German workmen, under armed guard, began erecting a barbed-wire fence that bisected the city by running along the borders of the American, British, and French sectors. The so-called 'Anti-Fascist Bulwark' ran down the middle of Bernauer Straße, through cemeteries, and skirted around the Brandenburg Gate. The surface of Ebert Straße was torn up to make vehicle access impossible. Meanwhile, dazed East Berliners were held in check by machine gun toting members of the People's Police. A West Berlin policeman watched the drama unfold. He later recalled his impressions of those first moments of Berlin's physical division, 'At first we thought that the East German Border Police were going to overrun us and march into West Berlin, but they remained precisely on the sector border, right down to the inch'. A Reuter's correspondent was on hand to witness the events of this momentous day:

> Early today I became the first person to drive an East Berlin car through the police cordons since the border controls began shortly after midnight. The clamp down was in full swing. The Brandenburg Gate, main crossing point between the two halves of the city, was surrounded by East German Police, some armed with sub-machine guns, and members of the para-military 'factory fighting groups'. West Berlin and

> West German cars were passing freely into East Berlin, in accordance with the new regulations. In contrast to my earlier failure to get through into West Berlin just after the borders had been temporarily sealed, my special green accreditation card this time gained me a free passage from a courteously smiling policeman. He told me: 'Nobody was allowed through for a period of time of about one hour in the middle of the night while we got in position. Now things are working as we mean them to go on, someone with a card like yours will not be prevented from going through. But you must take no East Germans with you'.
>
> I drove back through the gate and watched four West Berlin cars pass through after a policeman saluted and checked their identity cards. All asked questions, and explained the new regulations patiently. It appeared that the police were under strict instructions to try to avoid incidents. At one of the other thirteen checkpoints cars and pedestrians were being allowed through. Three cordons of police checked my passport as I walked through. The first cordon was armed with rifles or sub-machine guns, the second with revolvers and batons. The third group was unarmed. The security precautions nevertheless were on a large scale. All along the border about 100 yards back, armed police and factory workers were guarding buildings in pairs. I sighted one armed policeman gazing from a top-floor window. It is hard to see how the controls can be kept up at their present rate.

Kept up they were. Three days later, more workers arrived to construct a wall formed from concrete blocks. This structure was set back slightly from the original barbed wire fence. While the barbed wire fence didn't seem either formidable or permanent, the new structure was both.

Some elements of the West German press lamented that the physical division of Berlin had taken the Allies by surprise. Conrad Ahlers of the *Frankfurter Rundschau* wrote:

> So we are now standing before the ruin of a political strategy that was intended to bring freedom to the people of the GDR and reunification to the Germans. No one is likely to dare to introduce effective measures such as economic sanctions for fear of provoking a new Berlin blockade. The West is caught in a trap in Berlin that could slam shut at any minute. Negotiations are the only way out. It is now no longer merely a question of prudence, but also morality, that every attempt is made to undo what has happened, after previous policies have brought us to the brink of disaster.

The East German press also stressed the importance of negotiations. The *Neues Deutschland* noted with satisfaction:

East German Guard Conrad Schumann's leap to freedom. (*Wikimedia Commons*)

The Wall takes on a solid form.

> Three days after our justified measures, it has become apparent that they have been understood very well. People everywhere are beginning to understand that the balance of power has to be considered and that it is time to agree to negotiations. The peace-monitoring activities of our security forces on the borders of the GDR thus go towards accelerating negotiations. We banked on this effect, and we therefore welcome it with all our heart.

American policy-makers did not see the need to negotiate as the wall had not affected Allied access to West Berlin, their continued presence in the city, nor the right of West Berlin's citizens to self-determination. While Ulbricht and his Soviet masters had brutally cut the flow of refugees, they had not made any attempt to launch a new blockade. The American administration accepted the wall as the new reality, many young East Berliners did not.

On 24 August, a twenty-four-year-old tailor named Günter Litfin was shot and killed by a border guard while attempting to swim to freedom in the West. Litfin is known to have entered the Spree Canal (a branch of the River Spree) at the Humboldhafen Harbour. While not a particularly strong swimmer, he believed he had a good chance of success. However, Litfin's luck ran out when he was spotted by a member of the Transport Police (Trapo) who was standing on a railway bridge overlooking the Spandauer Schiffahrts Canal. Litfin was ordered to swim back to the Humboldhafen Harbour. Warning shots were fired by the Trapo to reinforce the point. Litfin pressed on. The Trapo fired again, the next shot hitting Litfin in the back of the head. His lifeless body lay still, tantalisingly close to his goal. Had he made the attempt the day before, he would have most likely succeeded. His only crime was bad timing, as a shoot to kill policy had been adopted by the authorities that very morning.

Meanwhile, the administration in Washington had been stirred into action by a direct appeal from the West Berlin mayor, Willy Brandt, who had loudly proclaimed, 'Berlin expects more than words, Berlin expects political action'. The American press reacted strongly against this 'mere mayor'. Kennedy was however determined to defend the trust that the citizens of West Berlin had placed in the Allies. He did so by risking confrontation with the Soviets by sending a convoy of 1,500 heavily armed troops along the autobahn route into West Berlin. Apart from being stopped and counted, the column proceeded unmolested to the Kurfürstendamm, where they received a rapturous welcome from the crowds which had gathered to meet them. At the same time, the aggressively confident and self-assertive General Clay and Vice President Lyndon B. Johnson arrived at Tempelhof to an equally warm reception.

All of West Berlin let out a collective sigh of relief, as the hoisting of the stars and stripes once again symbolised America's determination to hold firm.

A few weeks later, Clay set into motion a crisis which his superiors in Washington did not deem worth fighting over. Breaking with established quadripartite rules, East German border guards began to demand that Allied personnel present their passports. On 22 October, American diplomat Allan Lighter and his wife fell foul of these new formalities at Check Point Charlie. Clay reacted strongly by sending a combat squad to escort Lighter's car through the checkpoint with their bayonets fixed. During the following days, Clay despatched numerous armed parties into East Berlin to test the resolve of the East German authorities.

On 26 October, Clay upped the stakes by dispatching ten M-48 Patton tanks and three M-59 armoured personnel carriers to the Checkpoint Charlie area. The following morning, thirty-three Soviet T-54 tanks rolled into East Berlin. Ten of them took up position facing the American armour at Check Point Charlie. CBS news reporter Daniel Schorr witnessed the scene:

> The Cold War took on a new dimension tonight when American and Russian fighting men stood arrayed against each other for the first time in history. Until now, the East–West conflict had been waged through proxies—German and other. But tonight, the superpowers confronted each other in the form of ten low-slung tanks facing American Patton tanks less than a hundred yards apart....

For Clay, the issue was a matter of prestige following Washington's supine stance regarding the wall. Both sides put their forces in Europe on full alert, and for sixteen hours, the world waited with bated breath. Thankfully, common sense prevailed, as an agreement for mutual withdrawal was arranged through diplomatic back-channels. Clay had clearly overstepped the mark by acting unilaterally, the commander of American forces in Germany stating, 'What on earth did Clay think he was doing? You don't spit in the face of a bulldog'. Clay remained in Berlin for a few more months before being discreetly recalled to Washington.

Above: Soviet tanks in Berlin during the 1961 crisis. (*Wikimedia Commons*)

Left: General Lucius D. Clay. (*Wikimedia Commons*)

12

Jumping Into the Ring—Günter Grass

Günter Grass single-handedly forged a new era of post-war literature from the ruins of defeat and shame. His political irreverence angered both former Nazis who had made themselves comfortable during West Germany's economic transformation, and the East German Communists who regarded his views as heresy. The unrestrained sexual frankness in Grass's novels helped to usher in the social and sexual revolution in the late 1960s. Grass's adoptive home in Berlin's bohemian quarter was the crucible of a revolutionary social movement that later shook the city to its foundations.

Grass was born on 16 October 1927 in Danzig's Langfuhr district. His parents were lower middle-class merchants of German–Polish descent. He grew up in a modest two-room flat with shared toilet and kitchen facilities. There was very little living space, Grass later recalling that, 'My sister and I each had a niche under the window sills of the living room. That's where I put my books and my things'. At the age of sixteen, he became a Luftwaffe auxiliary. Grass then spent a few months with the Reich Labour Service before being drafted into the 10th Waffen SS Panzer Division *Frundsberg*. He served as an assistant tank gunner on the Eastern Front until he was wounded in action on 25 April 1945. He was later captured while recuperating at a military hospital in Marienbad by advancing American forces. Grass was then transferred to a prisoner of war camp in Bad Aibling.

From 1948 to 1952, he studied sculpture and graphics at the prestigious Düsseldorf Künstakademie. However, Grass regarded himself as being self-educated. 'I left school at the age of fifteen and I couldn't even spell properly when I began writing my first longer manuscript' he later recalled. Indeed, the manuscript for his first novel was littered with spelling mistakes. During the early 1950s, he penned a series of surrealistic self-illustrated poems, which were published under the title *The Advantages of Windfowl.* He also wrote a series of plays which reflected his interest in the more grotesque and bizarre aspects of life.

In 1959, Grass experienced his first commercial success with the surrealistic novel *The Tin Drum.* This grotesque and licentious tale of Oskar Matzerath's search for his true identity amidst the social and political upheavals of the National Socialist era scandalised the more conservative elements in German society. The mass-circulation newspaper *Bild* labelled Grass a 'petulant poet'. The West German president was even more outraged, stating that, 'Some of the things he writes are so lewd, that not even married couples would discuss them'. The regional assembly in Bremen refused to award Grass a literary prize awarded to him on the grounds that his novel was both blasphemous and obscene. Two years later, attempts were made to include the novel on a Federal Government list of materials likely to corrupt the minds of young people. By 1963, a total of twenty-four criminal charges had been levelled against Grass, all of them leading to nothing.

The success of *The Tin Drum* was crowned with the award of the Berlin Critics Prize in 1960. Grass moved to Berlin's bustling creative quarter located in Friedenau. Here, he completed the next two volumes of what came to be known as the Danzig Trilogy. The novels *Cat and Mouse* (1961) and *Dog Years* (1963) were a grotesquely eloquent and vivid *post facto* reimagining's of the National Socialist period. Literary success conferred accolades and wealth upon Grass. While he basked in the praise heaped upon him, Grass rejected the rampant consumerism that had come to characterise West German society. Emulating the Wandervogel movement of the late nineteenth century, Grass lived an anti-materialist lifestyle, refusing to own a car, television, or telephone.

On 14 August 1961, Grass wrote to Anna Seghers, chairperson of the German Democratic Republic Writers' Association. His unanswered letter drew parallels between the imprisonment of East Berliners behind the wall and Hitler's concentration camps. Two days later, Grass and novelist and poet Wolfdietrich Schnurre penned an open letter to all East German writers, declaring that 'barbed wire, machine-pistols and tanks are not the means to make conditions in East Germany bearable for the state's citizens. Only a state no longer sure of its citizens support tries to save itself in this way'. Stephan Hermlin, a close friend of Ulbricht, and one of the most influential writers in East Germany argued that the wall was a bulwark against neo-fascism. Heiner Müller, the East German dramatist, theatre director, poet, writer, and essayist stated that the wall was 'right and necessary', postulating that it facilitated 'a critical and realistic' new beginning for German culture.

Grass was already a well-known figure in East Germany, when his open criticism of the wall brought him to the attention of the Stasi. From then on, whenever he crossed into East Berlin, his activities were constantly monitored. Grass frequently gave readings of his works to writers' associations, publishers' representatives, and theatre people on the other side of the wall. He did not realise it at the time, but as Kai Schlüter, author of *Günter Grass in the Crosshairs* states, 'Grass was completely surrounded by spies when he came to the GDR. All his official interlocutors were unofficial informants, all of them'. These informers watched every move Grass made. This was not at all difficult, as Grass was such a well-known figure. The Stasi handlers gave their surveillance subject the codename 'Bolt', and meticulously recorded the details passed on to them by their informants. The Stasi were particularly interested in Grass because they regarded him as a dangerous Machiavellian character pursuing a political agenda that was regarded as an anathema in the rigidly controlled East German state.

The lifelong mistrust of advocates of revolutionary change held by Grass was understandable. During his formative years, he had experienced Nazi indoctrination in the Hitler Youth, and while toiling in a potash works as a member of the Reich Labour Service. Here, he saw at close quarters petty Nazi officials, embittered Communists, and disenfranchised Social Democrats. He later recounted:

> In the potash works I learned to live without ideology. I still had the morning ceremonies of the Hitler Youth in my ears, those Sunday attestations to the flag, swearing on blood and soil of course, and then there were the Communists attempting to entice me with similar relics dragged out of the lumber room of their ideology. As a child who had already been burnt, I stuck carefully to my taciturn Social Democrats who neither babbled of a thousand-year Reich nor world revolution, who in 1946 had already hurled the remaining ideological ballast into the dustbin.

For the rest of his life, Grass maintained the view that society could only be changed gradually by small steps. Ironically, this was the same method advocated by Stalin for the introduction of Communism by 'zigzags'. This 'life-affirming pessimist' had an ambivalent relationship with the Social Democrats who espoused a similar world view to his own. Grass maintained his political independence by refusing to join the party at this time.

In 1965, Grass hit the campaign trail in support of Willy Brandt. While still not a member of the party, this firebrand would certainly draw the crowds. Peter Brinkmann was one of the organisers of the so-called 'Grass Event' held in the conservative stronghold of Cloppenburg on 14 September. He later recalled, 'We wanted to do something different back then. And we got the one who creates the most friction'. However, some party members were less than impressed, Hans Lemp, the local Social Democrat candidate stating that, 'None of the local Social Democrat offices had any influence on the place and time of the event.... Personally, I do not identify myself with this event in any way, because my attitude to Grass neither accords with my views on life, nor my political convictions'. Lemp was certainly not alone, as few people in Cloppenburg were willing to hear Grass out.

In front of a largely hostile audience of 3,000 people at the Münsterlandhalle, Grass vainly attempted to preach his gospel. Fights and scuffles broke out amongst the audience, and the firebrand was pelted with eggs, tomatoes and ripe pears. Later, Grass lamented, 'Even reading from the New Testament would not have calmed the tumult. I responded to thrown eggs with references to squandered subsidies for agriculture'. Brinkmann however was more than happy with the chaos in the hall that night. The event was widely reported in the national press. He later recalled that, 'The first disturbed election campaign event in the history of the still young Federal Republic took place in Cloppenburg'. For Grass, the event served to cement his reputation for courting controversy; a reputation which he enjoyed enormously.

In his novels, plays, poems, essays, and newspaper interviews, Grass confronted his fellow Germans with uncomfortable truths about their wartime amnesia, their politics, and themselves. He later explained that his focus on Germany's past was born from the 'mountains of rubble and cadavers, fruit of the womb of German history. The more I shovelled, the more it grew. It simply could not be ignored'. However, for many years, Grass chose to ignore his own history. It was only in later life when his autobiography entitled *Peeling the Onion* was published, that he finally revealed his service in the Waffen SS. His disclosure unleashed a storm of protest. Joachim Fest, the renowned historian and biographer of Hitler said, 'I don't know how he could play this double role for so long'.

Having aligned himself with the leftist cause for so long, it was therefore no surprise that Grass's strongest critics came from conservative elements within the government. Wolfgang Börser, a Christian Democratic Union spokesperson told *Bild* that the person who had demanded so much of others should now 'make these demands on himself'. Grass addressed the criticism in a television interview in which he said, 'I've always thought about it, it was always present. And I was of the opinion that what I did as an author, as a citizen of this country, was the opposite of that which had shaped my youth during the Nazi era. For me, that sufficed'. Arguably, in this interview, Grass was acting as his own judge and jury, absolving himself of the burden of war guilt. His plea of mitigation is similar to that of Larry LaSalle in Robert Cormier's novel *Heroes* who asks, 'Does that one sin of mine wipe away all the good things?' Grass may have been driven by ego and the constant need for recognition, but he was essentially a product of his times. As the writer and publicist Ralph Giordano opined, 'What else could he have done during that time in the face of the Nazis' all-powerful propaganda apparatus? Nothing! I believed that he suffered terribly for keeping silent about this'. Indeed, what else could he have done?

As a political activist, Grass enjoyed courting controversy. Indeed, he seemed willing to dive head first into any kind of political confrontation, no matter what the personal consequences. However, it is as a writer that Grass will best be remembered. For years he struggled to replicate the enormous impact of his early works. His continued efforts eventually bore fruit some forty years after the publication of *The Tin Drum* with the award of the Nobel Prize for Literature. The academy's citation concluded, 'Mr Grass goes deeper than most and he unearths the intertwined roots of good and evil'. Roger Cohen of *The New York Times* further elucidated on this theme by stating:

> Perhaps in no other country but Germany, home to Goethe and Goebbels, to Heine and Hitler, is this intertwining so intense. The

Günter Grass. (*Wikimedia Commons*)

> author's authority has lain in his power to imbue his prose with a matching intensity. As Mr Grass writes in 'Dog Years', 'While God was still at school, in the heavenly playground he came up with the idea of creating the world, together with his schoolmate, the talented little devil. This devil moreover was powerful, seductive to a conformist nation, and often cleverly disguised....'

While Grass has been compared to Thomas Mann, the two writers came from very different backgrounds. His obituary in the German newspaper *Spiegel* noted that 'nothing could have been more alien to Grass than Mann's affluent and bourgeois milieu. There was something plebeian about the rowdy, clear words with which Grass jumped into the ring throughout his life'. More than anything, Grass rescued German literature from the linguistic and moral destruction of the National Socialist era which created nothing of any great artistic worth.

13

Aggression in Felt Slippers

The concrete symbol of division running through and around Berlin created an uneasy peace in which Cold War certainties became established. West Berlin's mayor Willi Brandt was quick to recognise the new reality, and equally quick to recognise that the wall was no more than 'a show of weakness and fear, not force'. Therefore, if the wall could not be physically removed, everything should be done to make it as permeable as possible. The first step in this process was to gain the trust of the East German authorities. Brandt declared his intentions to his close colleagues:

> The East German people are the worst ones affected by the GDR's financial policies, which are aimed at defending the GDR against us. If we want to make life better for our brothers and sisters, we need to relax the tension and convince the East German leaders to trust us. By condemning the communist regime's need for defence, we can 'soften' it gradually, and allow the GDR to prosper economically, rather than staying in its current impoverished state.

The idea behind Brandt's relaxation of tension was highly subversive, the overall aim being not to support the East German regime, but to gradually undermine its legitimacy. The East German regime understood Brandt's aims perfectly. Indeed, the East German minister for foreign affairs, Otto Winzer, referred to the policy as 'aggression in felt slippers'. Fearing that Brandt's initiative would appeal to their Soviet comrades, the Stasi issued a warning to, 'never underestimate the growing dangers of social democracy and revisionism'. The KGB chose to ignore this warning as they were in favour of fostering a more progressive relationship with the Bonn government. The moribund Soviet economy needed assistance.

Uri Andropov, the cooly calculating and ambitious head of the KGB was convinced that the powerhouse West German economy could help to modernise the backwards Soviet economic-industrial complex. Notwithstanding, the KGB's lack of opposition to his scheme, Brandt and his representative Egon Bahr had to tread carefully. While the KGB may have been in favour of closer economic ties with West Germany, the Communist leadership remained deeply suspicious of Brandt's motives. Moreover, negotiations would have to be conducted through back-channels, as any direct contact with the East German leadership would be construed as an acknowledgement of the Ulbricht regime. Progress was slow, but eventually an agreement was reached to allow Berlin families separated by the physical division of the city to reunite, albeit briefly.

After lengthy negotiations, the 'Border Crossing Agreement' was eventually signed on 18 December 1963. This agreement allowed the citizens of West Berlin to visit their families on the other side of the wall over the Christmas and New Year period. Obtaining a permit was a long and complicated process. One elderly woman later recalled:

> We used to sit down together every day. Since the wall was built, I've been all alone in West Berlin. I have needed a lot of strength to survive these past two years... I stood in line for three days to get three pass permits. I'll line up again, even if it takes longer.

Despite the bureaucratic rigmarole, Brandt regarded the agreement as a spectacular success, with over 800,000 people crossing the border between 19 December 1963 and 5 January 1964. The West Berlin mayor then went on television to praise the value of taking action rather than 'making ourselves comfortable in the trenches of this war of words we have been waging for the last few years'. Not everyone was happy with this new direction. The newspaper baron Axel Springer published a number of stinging articles in the influential *Bild Zeitung* criticising what he saw as Brandt's abandonment of Germany's 'national' interest. Nonetheless, Brandt's popularity effectively shielded him from such criticism, allowing him to proceed with his policies relatively unhindered. By the end of the decade, Brandt's new direction had ushered in the transformative era of Ostpolitik.

14

Mitte-Moabit-Gesundbrunnen-Alexanderplatz-Friedrichshain-Kreuzberg Viewpoints

Viewpoint (C1): DDR Mural and 17 June 1953 Memorial (Platz des Volksaufstandes von 1953, Berlin)

Design and Architectural Features

On 10 August 1950, six artists were invited to submit ideas for a new large-scale mural to adorn the House of Ministries. After considering the various ideas put forward, the artist Max Lingner was invited to create a piece of public art depicting the contented citizens of the German Democratic Republic looking confidently towards a bright future. Lingner's original concept was entitled 'The Importance of Peace for the Cultural Development of Humanity and the need to fight for it'. This rather pretentious appellation was rejected, as was the accompanying design depicting a grouping of contented families enjoying the benefits of the worker's paradise. Prime Minister Otto Grotewohl who had originally commissioned the mural wanted a design with stronger political undertones. During the design process, he insisted on five revisions, ultimately resulting in an approved version which bore little resemblance to Lingner's original concept.

For many years, Lingner had worked in Paris. As such, his work was regarded by the authorities in Berlin as, 'Too French'. The frivolous and playful aspects of his work were at odds within the austere and humourless milieu in which he attempted to practice his art. The final version approved by Grotewohl was a highly stylised piece in which members of the youth organisation, musicians, young pioneers, officials, tradesmen, farmers, engineers, builders, and intellectuals can be seen working together for the common cause. Their fixed smiles create a somewhat sinister impression, reminiscent of the ostentatiously happy multitudes who can be seen

A section of Lingner's mural depicting life in the worker's paradise.

exercising their discipline and devotion in Kim Jong-un's North Korea. However, there was a price to pay for the enforced abandonment of artistic integrity as neither Grotewohl nor Lingner were satisfied with the finished mural. Indeed, the artist was said to be so repulsed by the design that he could not bear to look at it. Lingner was right to look away, as by the time the mural was completed, the happy and contented faces depicted on its Meissen tiles contrasted sharply with the grim reality of life in East Germany.

Wolfgang Rüppel's memorial to the popular uprising of 17 June 1953 contrasts sharply with the over-stylised propagandistic mural by Lingner. The small square on which it is located was designed by the architect Ute Piroeth. The location provides a strong visual link in which the ideational requirements of Lingner's mural contrast sharply with the quasi-ornamental effect produced by Rüppel's processed digital image. In order to view the image, visitors need to look at it from an angle. The double transfer of the image onto two overlapping glass surfaces serves to create an image which stretches the limits of readability and intelligibility. If the 'Building the Republic' mural was all about readability, then the memorial to the 17 June 1953 uprising ensnares the viewer in a process of interpretation and validation.

Viewpoint (C2): Berlin Wall Section (Niederkirchnerstraße, 1, Berlin)

Providing a 'universal' description of the Berlin Wall is always a challenge. Over a period of twenty-eight years, the 'elaborate and ever-changing system of obstacles' known as the 'the' Berlin Wall became a potent Cold War symbol. Yet, when we think of 'the' wall, what images immediately come to mind? The image of border guard Conrad Schumann making his leap to freedom over a simple barbed-wire fence on 15 August 1961? Or perhaps, the image of families physically separated by the concrete monstrosity that ran along Bernauer Straße? The four generations of the border structure progressed towards a coherent 'wall' image. Perhaps that image was strongest in the West, where the smooth, flat surface of the fourth-generation structure produced an impression of solidity and permanency. Yet, to reach this stage of evolution, 'the' wall went through several incarnations.

The first incarnation of the border defence system was not a wall at all, but a makeshift barrier consisting of concertina wire and fencing hastily erected on 13 August 1961. Four days later, the first-generation wall began to take shape. This solid structure consisted mostly of square cinderblock elements that when cemented together produced a two-metre high wall. For would be escapees, the best chance of reaching the West was while the situation at border crossing points was still relatively fluid. On one day in September 1961, fifty-three people reached West Berlin, six of them by swimming across the River

The Berlin Wall running along Niederkirchner Straße *c.* 1988. (*Wikimedia Commons*)

Havel. For several weeks after the wall went up, border guards were reported by escapees as having either simply looked the other way, or as having fired a few warning shots to draw suspicion away from themselves. However, the border situation would not remain fluid for long. Would-be escapees would be forced to come up with more and more inventive and audacious plans if they were to have any chance of success.

On 10 October 1961, East German photographer Horst Beyer made a successful dash to freedom in the West. His plan hinged on managing to convince the authorities that he should be responsible for producing a publicity stunt on the border to celebrate the twelfth anniversary of Ulbricht's regime. The authorities took the bait. Beyer then activated his plan by arranging for the photo-shoot to be carried out on a less well defended border area. The photo-shoot would consist of a bevy of beauties from a Communist women's sports team presenting border guards with bouquets of flowers. The border guards would be somewhat distracted by all the attention, allowing Beyer to make his move. He took photo after photo, each time moving the group a little closer to the white line on the road which marked the border. When one of the border guards called out, 'Be careful that you don't step across the line', Beyer took his cue. Springing into action, Beyer made a dash for the West. Most of the border guards were too distracted to react quickly enough. The one who had warned him was simply too dumbstruck to do anything about it.

A few weeks later, East German schoolteacher Fritz Berger executed a successful escape by impersonating an American officer at the Checkpoint Charlie crossing. His 'uniform' consisted of a pair of khaki work pants, an old German military shirt, a Czech tunic, Russian shoulder boards, and various items of wartime era American insignia. While this motley collection of uniform items and accessories would not have passed muster on a parade ground, it was convincing enough to fool the border guards who could not begin to conceive of such an audacious attempt at escape. Berger's affected nonchalance added a degree of authenticity to his disguise. With a friendly wave from the border guards, Berger was allowed to simply stroll across the border.

While some escape attempts involved a high degree of inventiveness and audacity, most relied on the direct application of force. Motor vehicles remained the weapon of choice for most would be escapers. With some modification, any large vehicle could be used as a battering ram to break through the border defences. At a meeting of the Central Team for the construction of the wall held five weeks after 'Barbed wire Sunday', it was revealed that there had been 216 forced breakthroughs involving 417 people. The meeting was chaired by Erich Honecker who addressed the issue directly by stating:

> A complete evacuation or more rapid evacuation of unreliable elements must take place in the streets of Berlin and the environs of Berlin adjacent to West Berlin where the border line runs alongside houses where people could still climb out using ropes. Firearms are to be used against traitors and violators. Measures are to be taken to allow criminals to be caught in the 100-metre restricted area. Space for observation and shooting is to be created in the restricted area. Managers of collective farms must be informed that only low-standing crops are to be planted in the restricted area. The evacuation of hostile and unreliable elements must be stepped-up.

Stepped-up they were. By the following year, the second-generation wall had begun to emerge. This wall was in reality no more than an improvement upon the existing wall, with many of the cinderblock elements being replaced by concrete slabs. However, it represented a definite improvement in terms of border security.

The third-generation wall which emerged in 1965 was a more formidable structure comprised of 'fairly narrow concrete slabs inserted horizontally between H-sectioned posts of reinforced concrete'. The wall was topped-off with lengths of concrete sewage pipe. The 200 metres of wall remaining on Niederkirchnerstraße represent a fourth-generation structure known as 'Grenzmauer 75' (Border Wall 75). As the title suggests, work on updating the basic infrastructure commenced in the mid-1970s.

Border Wall 75 consisted of approximately 45,000 pre-cast concrete L-shaped wall segments. The vertical outer face of each segment faced the West, with the inner L-shaped aspect facing east. The eastern facing aspect was shaped in such a way as to make it virtually impossible for would be escapers to gain a foothold. The top of each segment was crowned with a cylindrical asbestos-concrete tube which made getting a handhold equally problematical. In *The Secret Life of Buildings* Edward Hollis describes the new structure's elaborate defensive systems:

> The concrete slabs formed the western face of Grenzmauer 75. Behind them was a row of tank traps. Behind the tank traps was a ditch. Behind the ditch was a patrol track for vehicles, and then a marching track for infantry. Behind the marching track there was a row of street lamps, and behind the street lamps was a row of watchtowers. Behind the watchtowers was a barbed-wire corridor inhabited by attack dogs, and then a low-tension electric fence. Behind the electric fence was a 'fakir's bed' of nails that protruded from the ground, and another concrete wall. Behind this rear wall was a border area cleared of buildings....

These increasingly sophisticated border and zonal defences were not impenetrable but made the business of escape a serious and potentially costly endeavour. Between 1961–1989, approximately 140 people were either shot by border guards, or died as a result of accidents or suicide.

In 1990, the remaining section of the wall on Niederkirchnerstraße was declared a historical monument. It is now part of the 'Overall Concept of the Berlin Wall' preservation and commemoration project being developed by the Berlin Senate. The protected status conferred on this section of wall will hopefully ensure that it remains a tangible symbol of the Cold War for many years to come.

Viewpoint (C3): Checkpoint Charlie (Friedrichstraße, 43-45, Berlin)

Allied Check Point C, or Checkpoint Charlie as it is better known, was originally a simple wooden structure which reflected the Allied view that the Berlin Wall was neither a permanent nor legitimate border. While there were other crossing points in and around Berlin, Checkpoint Charlie was notable for its city centre location on Friedrichstraße. Allied military personnel monitored diplomatic and military traffic, but were also on hand to register and offer advice to travellers venturing into East Berlin. These non-diplomatic and non-military travellers were often subjected to intense security checks at the more elaborate East German checkpoint before being allowed to pass through. Border guards were particularly interested in any newspapers or literature which criticised conditions in the worker's paradise.

The iconic checkpoint was the scene of some audacious escape attempts, some of which were spectacularly successful. Heinz Meixner's dash under the border vehicle barrier 1963 has become the stuff of legend. Meixner was an Austrian citizen working as a lathe operator in West Germany. As a foreigner, he was able to enjoy reasonably unfettered access into East Berlin. On one such visit in September 1962, he met, and then subsequently fell in love with a petite young East German named Margarete Thurau. Having unsuccessfully petitioned the authorities in East Berlin for an exit visa, Heinz and Margarete became increasingly determined that a bankrupt ideology backed up by concrete and steel would not stop the course of their true love.

Meixner came up with a daring plan to get his future wife and mother-in-law out of East Germany. As he could not drive through the vehicle crossing barrier at Checkpoint Charlie with two East Germans on board, he would drive under it. He began to visit car hire companies in West Berlin in the hope of finding a car with a low enough profile for the plan to work. Eventually, he settled on a red Austin Healey Sprite sports convertible. Next, he carried out a reconnaissance of the East German side of Checkpoint Charlie. Feigning engine trouble, he was able to stop close enough to the vehicle barrier to estimate that letting some air out of the tyres and removing the windshield would give him sufficient clearance.

Shortly after midnight on 5 May, Meixner's red convertible approached the first checkpoint on the eastern side of Friedrichstraße. He managed to secrete his intended in the small space behind the driver's seat. His future mother in law's hiding place in the car was even more uncomfortable as she was forced to adopt a foetal position in the cramped boot. The waiting border guard motioned Meixner's car towards the customs shed. It was now or never.

Seizing the moment, Meixner put his foot down hard on the accelerator. He then skilfully negotiated the vertical steel barriers ahead. Then, when he reached the final horizontal barrier, he ducked down low as the car thundered under at high speed. Following his dash to freedom, he told reporters:

> I figured it would take the Vopos three seconds to draw their weapons once they realised what I was doing. But I thought that I could make it in those three seconds. Besides, we had thirty bricks behind Mrs Thurau to protect her if firing started. I felt I could make it with about three inches to spare. Now we can get married.

Little did Meixner know it, but his escape would be replicated a few months later in the very same car, still bearing the original number plate. While the East German authorities had noted the make and model of car used, they were still blissfully unaware of the Sprite's surprisingly roomy interior.

Norbert Konrad was an Argentinian citizen working in Berlin as a radio mechanic. Like Meixner, he met and fell in love with an East German woman whose father was a staunch Communist. Having been refused an exit visa, Konrad planned an escape on similar lines to that attempted in May. He later recalled:

> I had four pillow cases which I had filled with sand and a big plate of marble. I broke up the plate and used it together with the sandbags to line the trunk in case one of the guards fired on us. Then Helga got in and I closed the trunk, but she screamed and I opened it again. Helga was crying and said she could not get any air. I told her that if she loved me she would get in.

A loose exhaust pipe almost scuppered the plan, but at 03:10 hrs on 29 July, the Sprite convertible reached the first red and white striped barrier.

Konrad's girlfriend later recounted the almost unbearable tension to reporters, 'I heard a guard ask Norbert for his passport and I stuffed a handkerchief into my mouth because I feared I would scream and I had to have something to bite on. I was sweating with fear'. After waiting for what seemed like an eternity behind a truck, border guards signalled the car to approach the customs shed. Konrad later recounted to reporters what happened next:

> I just pressed down on the gas pedal and drove through the slalom course at about thirty-five miles an hour. As I came through the slalom a guard almost got in the way but he jumped aside and I ripped the windshield off and pulled my head in before driving under the last two barriers.

Only later did it register in Konrad's mind that he had used the very same car as Meixner. Somewhat astonished by this revelation, Konrad was heard to say:

> An English friend had told me about the Austrian's escape, but he didn't have full details and I had not read the story at the time. After we made it and I saw a picture of the story. I realised that it was the same car. I almost fainted.

There would however be no more such escapes, as shortly afterwards East German border guards welded steel rods to the barrier. With the development of more effective counter-escape measures, the prospect of getting through the border defences at Checkpoint Charlie by bluff, deception, or the application of brute force diminished considerably.

The public and painful death of escapee Peter Fechter near the Checkpoint Charlie border crossing on 17 August 1962 underscored the inhumanity of the East German regime. At the same time, this tragedy served to highlight the political paralysis and indifference of the American administration. Newspaper photographer Wolfgang Bera who was on the scene asked an American soldier on duty to help Fechter, only to be told, 'It's not our problem'. Fechter's death was covered widely in the West German press. Coverage was highly critical of the lack of intervention by the Americans. In the popular newspaper *Bild,* the damning headline said, 'VoPos let 18-year-old bleed to death—As Americans watch'. Meanwhile in Washington, President Kennedy discussed the matter with the Secretary of State Dean Rusk:

> Kennedy—What plans do we have for handling similar situations?
> Rusk—Well, we have some for larger episodes.
> Kennedy—What about a single episode like this, though?

> Rusk-No one case is like another… For example, our people don't fish them out of canals. That's handled on the eastern side… I think perhaps the mistake that was made locally was not offering some medical care (to Fechner).
> Kennedy—Yeah… Of course, the West Berliners are not very generous but… that's all right. I think we just have to ride through this one.

Effectively, 'riding through this one' meant that American soldiers would continue to stand idly by while escapees were murdered. Their hands were tied by bureaucratic red tape which prevented them from assisting escapees on the eastern side of the wall.

In August 1989, would-be escaper Hans Spitzner found an American soldier in East Berlin who was willing to help him flee to the West along with Peggy, his seven-year-old daughter. Spitzner had previously fallen foul of the authorities for refusing to follow party orders in an election. He later recalled his feelings about living in East Germany's repressive society:

> It is hard to describe how life was so hard and dreary. The ache to get away from the Stasi police snoops, from the grey meat, from the clothes that itched and the air that stung your eyes was palpable… I was paralysed and feeble. I felt completely exposed, but I was strong inside and not willing to give up. I had not committed any crimes and did not

Checkpoint Charlie *c.* 1965. (*Wikimedia Commons*)

> feel guilty at all, yet still I cannot deny a feeling of fear. I was inferior to these people; the psychological pressure was enormous.

After his wife Ingrid had been granted permission to visit an Aunt in Austria, the idea of escaping, an idea they had discussed many times, became more real. Spitzner's plan was simplicity itself, as there was, 'No tunnel, no balloon, no pole-vault'. He later told reporters about how he hatched the plan and then set it in motion:

> The idea of escaping in the trunk of a car came to my mind while reading an article in the newspaper *Junge Welt.* I read that there was an official instruction that said members of the Allied military forces were not to be searched. Only the usual passport check was conducted. In the case of reasonable suspicion of a flight risk the car was surrounded and the occupants forced out, it wasn't until then that they could be arrested since the inside of the vehicle was de facto American territory.
>
> My wife was already in Austria (it was common practice to allow a member of the family to leave briefly as long as others stayed behind as potential hostages) and this encouraged me to try to escape and not have to expose my wife to the risk. She and my daughter did not know anything specific about my plans. Shortly before, I prepared my daughter in a playful way. While on our way to Berlin, I passed it off to her as a kind of hide and seek game… I felt panic and fear; it was life threatening. I was totally aware of being caught, but the urge to live in a free country gave me the strength to try it over and over again. I wanted to escape the system and wanted to give it the cold shoulder. I wanted to demonstrate that its power could not keep everybody from leaving.
>
> I wanted to meet a soldier who was driving a car, and I also tried my luck with bus drivers. Peggy was always by my side, this made me less suspicious, and a child was rather inconspicuous to the authorities. I felt powerless and was sad every time I was rejected. But it was a special kind of challenge indeed, dangerous and special, and this is why I did not give up. I have always been the warrior type who pursues his goals to the end and does not give up that quickly.

For two days, Spitzner made dangerous approaches to American soldiers in East Berlin, never knowing if he was being observed by the Stasi. He was about to give up when he spotted a black Toyota Camry with American number plates. He determined to have one more try.

The black car was parked on Karl-Marx-Allee. Seizing the moment, Spitzner approached the driver, a young Sergeant named Eric Yaw. With his heart thumping, Spitzner gestured towards the American. This was it, the moment of truth. It was now or never:

> He was hesitant, but to my delight he opened the car window which allowed me to make my request. When he agreed first I thought that he had misunderstood, because I could not believe that he would take on such a burden, that he would, at the risk of his life and knowing that he was breaching official instructions to help me and my daughter. I was a little confused and very, very excited at the time.

Sergeant Yaw motioned Spitzner and his daughter to get into the boot of the car. It was a hot August day, and the drive to the border crossing seemed like an eternity. In a newspaper interview given twenty years after the fall of Communism, Spitzner recounted the confused thoughts going through his mind as he lay in the boot of Yaw's car:

> In the trunk many thoughts crossed my mind. On the one hand I did not want to be caught by the border policeman, because that would have meant prison for me, and my daughter would have been taken to an unknown place, probably a state community home or to new parents who were loyal to the party. I was scared, anxious, and pictured many scenarios. It was like a thunderstorm in my head, I was unable to think straight. I was shivering with fear. Of course, I knew about the firing orders and the cruel methods the civil servants used against people who tried to escape, everybody in the GDR knew about this.

Meanwhile, Peggy remained strangely calm as the black car made its way towards Checkpoint Charlie:

> I was not nervous. I even calmed my father down in the trunk of Eric's car. He tried to talk to me to avoid me getting scared, but I told him that we could not speak or someone might hear us. Of course, I could not estimate the scope of this undertaking, but I knew that it was important to my family and my dad that we got where we wanted to go safely and therefore I had to listen to my dad and be brave.

After approximately twenty-five minutes, the car came to a halt at the border crossing. The tension must have been unbearable at this point as the border guards were known to use infrared scanners to detect escapees. Surely they would be discovered.

If the car driven by Sergeant Yaw had been white, the escape attempt would have almost certainly failed. However, they were fortunate to have been travelling in a black car, as the paintwork absorbed so much heat that it rendered the scanners useless. When the car boot was finally opened, it was a smiling (and somewhat relieved) Sergeant Yaw who said, 'We're in the West. You can get out now'. Spitzner's daughter Peggy later recalled her impressions of those first precious hours of freedom in the West:

> My first memory is the trunk opening. I saw a big red brick building. Eric had taken us there because some of his friends lived there. He asked everybody in the building to donate clothes as my dad had forgotten to pack some for me. Later we were driving through Berlin, and while we were waiting at the traffic lights somewhere, a guy came to our open window who was promoting some kind of strawberry lemonade. He gave one to me for free. This was a completely new experience for me, I was over the moon. Usually, I went to the stores with adults and we were waiting in a queue for hours. Nobody just came to you and offered you stuff.

With his wife due to return to East Germany, it was imperative that Spitzner got a message through to her about his successful escape. He did so just in time as she was already packed and ready to leave for home in East Germany the next day. She flew instead to West Berlin, where a tearful, but joyous family reunion awaited her. Little did they know it, but they were to be the last East Germans to escape via Checkpoint Charlie. Three months later the wall which Spitzner once described as a 'razorblade in the flesh of the German folk' fell following the collapse of Communism. All Germans were now free.

The commercialisation of Checkpoint Charlie.

Viewpoint (C4): Haus am Checkpoint Charlie (Friedrichstrasse, 43-45, Berlin)

The museum known as Haus am Checkpoint Charlie was established by human rights activist Rainer Hildebrandt. In 1948, Hildebrandt founded the 'Taskforce Against Inhumanity' which strongly opposed the policies of the Soviet occupation forces before the official founding of the German Democratic Republic. Following the construction of the Berlin Wall, Hildebrandt founded the 13 August Working Group which fought against human rights violations resulting from the physical division of Berlin. On 19 October 1962, Hildebrandt opened an art exhibition in a small flat on Bernauer Straße. The object of the exhibition was to appeal to visitors to 'look through the uniform', and by doing so recognise that the border guards were people too. Hildebrandt's policy of humanising these instruments of oppression paid off to some degree as, 'Some of these border guards felt we had understood their predicament, and after fleeing the East, they came to work with us'. On 14 June 1963, the exhibit moved to its present location next to Checkpoint Charlie. The 13 August Working Group was registered with the city authorities as an association the following month. Haus am Checkpoint Charlie was characterised by an unconventional exhibition style, with objects being displayed without the typical organisation found in most museums. Grateful escapees donated escape equipment including their specially adapted cars. Some of the more interesting donations included Hans Strelczyk and Günter Wetzel's home-made hot air balloon and Manfred Burmeister's rather Heath Robinson-esque underwater scooter.

Over time, the museum developed a focus on non-violent protest. Museum exhibits collected by Hildebrandt included the typewriter on which the call for human rights (Charter 77) was prepared in Czechoslovakia, Mahatma Ghandi's sandals and diaries, and the death mask of the Russian dissident Andrey Sakharov. These exhibits continued to be displayed in the same unconventional style, prompting critics to argue that Hildebrandt had essentially amassed a private collection, not a museum. The site also served as a base for political activity where escapes were planned. It boasted a library, publishing facilities, and spaces for films and lectures. Government grants and tax breaks helped to fund the operation which was regarded as a valuable tool in the ideological war against Communist oppression.

Following the fall of Communism, Hildebrandt's third wife Alexandra reinvented the museum as 'a place of experience'. It operated on strict business principles, soon becoming one of the most commercially successful visitor attractions in Berlin. In 2002, the 13 August Working

Group gave up its status as an association. This action was a response to what Alexandra Hildebrandt saw as a lack of appreciation on the part of the authorities. Notwithstanding the museum's new status as a private entity, she went on to publicly stress that it was still essentially a civic enterprise:

> If we build a memorial on the street, with our own strength, without applying for tax funds, you have to be happy and grateful, and thank us for this. This is not private remembrance, this is public... There is civic engagement, but there is no private remembrance. There is civic remembrance and there are memorials built by the state.

An alternate interpretation of the museum is provided by Jenny Wüstenberg who makes the point in her recent book *Civic Society and Memory in Postwar Germany* that rather than being a civic enterprise, Haus an Checkpoint Charlie is a purely-for-profit venture which does not fit into a 'coherent landscape' of commemoration. While that may indeed be so, the museum's civic and political roots cannot be ignored, and today it still remains an important site in terms of memorialisation and remembrance.

The museum is open seven days a week. The doors open at 09:00 hrs and close late in the evening at 22:00 hrs. There is a cafe and shop on site. Tickets can be bought on the day, although booking in advance is advised as the site can get very busy.
Web: info@mauermuseum.de

Viewpoint (C5): Günter Litfin Memorial (Kieler Strasse, 2, Berlin)

Design and Architectural Features

The tragic death of Günter Litfin on 24 August 1961 is commemorated on a plaque attached to a former command tower which stands close to the Berlin–Spandau Ship Canal and the Invalid's Cemetery. The thirty-two command towers and 280 watchtowers in Berlin were designed by the Central Design and Construction Office. They were built to standard designs from precast concrete sections. The command tower on Kieler Straße is a type FüSt BT 4 × 4 which originally consisted of a basement, ground floor cells, first floor guard accommodation, a second-floor observation platform, and a roof area mounting a searchlight.

The site becomes a memorial

After the fall of the Berlin Wall there was an understandable clamour to remove all traces of the oppressive East German regime. Now, only two former command towers remain; the one on Kieler Straße, and the other at Schlesischer Busch, close to Treptower Park. In 2003, the mayor of Berlin, Klaus Wowereit told Jürgen Litfin (Günter Litfin's younger brother) about the abandoned tower which now stands on Kieler Straße. Jürgen remained grateful for the mayor's help, stating that 'Wowie helped me a lot in getting things rolling and acquiring all the necessary permissions. And now the tower is a listed building'. Under his stewardship, the site has gone from strength to strength. The well-planned exhibition has attracted visitors from all over the world. However, engaging with local schools has proved more of a problem. Perhaps that situation will improve in the future as more and more German school groups appear to be actively seeking out and visiting sites connected with their country's turbulent past.

The tower is now an established part of the Berlin Wall trail, although Jürgen refuses to allow any groups involved in the popular 'Trabi Safari' to enter as he finds the nostalgia and fetishisation of the DDR period highly distasteful. He had this to say about the current romanticisation of the DDR period:

> Everyone in charge of the DDR were all bastards. I don't think you can view or understand East Germany without looking at who ran it. Young people especially seem not to understand all those connections.

Perhaps he has a point, as in the rush to commercialise the imagery of the East German state, the repression and crimes of that regime have been relegated to the background.

All visits to this site are by appointment only. Due to the cramped nature of the site, Jürgen reserves the right to restrict admittance on particularly hot days. The island on which the tower now stands is surrounded by a sea of new and recent developments which reflect the ongoing gentrification of large areas of Berlin. Nonetheless, it remains an important Cold War site, one which this author does not hesitate to recommend.

Web: www.gedenkstaette-guenter-litfin.de

The Günter Litfin Memorial and Watchtower.

Viewpoint (C6): The Berlin Wall Memorial Ensemble on Bernauer Strasse

Architectural and Design Features

In April 1994, the German National Museum (with the full backing of the federal government) sponsored a competition to build a Berlin Wall memorial on the iconic Bernauer Straße site. In July 1995, it was announced that the competition had been won by the Stuttgart-based architects Claudia and Sven Kohlhoff. Their concept was to use artistic means to integrate and visually enhance the remaining border fortifications along Bernauer Straße. The monument was completed and dedicated in 1998. The following year, a documentation centre opened across the street in a remodelled building dating from 1965. It could be argued that the repurposing of an existing building demonstrated that the memorialisation of the wall was still peripheral to Holocaust remembrance.

The ensemble was completed in 2000 by the Chapel of Reconciliation, a clay-built structure designed by architects Rudolf Reitermann and Peter Sassenroth, and supervised by the clay artist Martin Rauch. This was the first clay built public building to be completed in Germany for 150 years, and the nation's first ever clay built church. The chapel 'stands as a triumph against its predecessor's destruction'. This modern building is

The Berlin Wall Museum on Bernauer Straße

a fine example of ecologically responsible construction. It also serves to unite the concept of 'green' architecture with remembrance.

In 2014, a new open-air exhibition opened to the public. The well-presented exhibition space contains texts, images, audio recordings, videos, and graphics. The various media employed in the exhibition space serve to explain the wall to visitors and to unite the 'loose constellation of wall-related sites' which make up the ensemble. The memorial site is an excellent example of responsiveness to visitor requirements and the need to stay relevant as memory culture continues to develop.

Documentation Centre: Open Tuesday—Sunday 10:00 hrs–18:00 hrs.
Open-Air Exhibition & Memorial Grounds: Open Monday—Sunday 08:00 hrs–22:00 hrs.
Chapel of Reconciliation: Prayer Services Tuesday–Friday 12:00 hrs–12:15 hrs.
Web: www.info@berliner-mauer-gedenkstaette.de

15

Tilting at Socialist Windmills—Erich Mielke

The Ministry for State Security was established on 8 February 1950 with the unanimous approval of the East German parliament. The Stasi came into being ten days later when their official status was confirmed by President Pieck. The relationship between the Stasi and the state was made explicit at the third-party congress held in June 1950. During this congress, the dual nature of the Stasi's tasks were clearly defined. The organs of state security were to 'unmask and eliminate the enemies of the working class and agents of imperialism'. The Stasi's immediate task was to discipline Social Democrats. Their forced merger with the Communists was deeply resented and as such they were regarded as an unreliable and subversive element. The subsequent destruction of all sources of political dissent led to the creation of a 'politbureaucracy' in which the party controlled all the levers of power. As the 'sword and shield' of the party, the Stasi was the instrument of state oppression which moulded East German society into an amorphous mass of obedient slaves.

Soviet agents and advisors were omnipresent during the Stasi's formative years. These 'friends' often participated in high level meetings of the organs of state security. Their participation inevitably led to friction. At a staff meeting in 1953, the minister for state security Ernst Wollweber made it clear that East German agents should always defer to their masters by stating that, 'If a Soviet instructor intervenes ... you can show that you have a mind of your own, but you have to follow the advice of the instructor'. These Soviet advisors also directed large-scale operations, including the 'Blitz' operation conducted between December 1954 and April 1955. The operation netted 188 American agents, 105 British agents, 100 West German agents, and 132 members of resistance organisations. As the numbers suggest, this operation largely focused on external threats. However, the East German leadership was more concerned with internal threats. The pervasive Soviet influence on Stasi policy led many in the East German Central Committee to question where exactly the Stasi's loyalties lay. The situation was ultimately resolved by the removal of Kremlin confidant Wollweber and his replacement by staunch party man Erich Mielke. This action served to reorientate Stasi policy towards internal repression.

In January 1958, Mielke made his report to the Central Committee plenum. His conclusions echoed the reorientation of party policy away from de-Stalinisation and towards more repressive measures to counteract 'ideological subversion', defined by Mielke as 'the enemy's method aimed at the party's disintegration in order to eliminate its leading role in building socialism and to soften up the GDR and the entire socialist camp'. Moscow's anti-Stalinist 'revisionism' under Khrushchev was seen as political heresy by the East German leadership. As such, the political reorientation of the Stasi was now directed towards stifling all forms of political dissent. Even the most carefully worded criticisms of the regime were now classed as 'subversion'.

Under Mielke's leadership the Stasi directed most of its activities towards domestic surveillance. As he saw it, the Stasi's main task was to ward off western ideological influence, which he classified as 'political-ideological diversion'. A combination of insecurity and political dogmatism led Mielke to expand his organisation. In 1956, there were 16,000 people employed by the Ministry of State Security. By 1961, that figure had risen to 20,000. However, it must be explained that the growth of the state security organisation was not a direct result of internal crises. The expansion of the Stasi after the construction of the Berlin Wall was relatively small. The social revolutions of 1968 shook the confidence of state security organisations in Moscow and Berlin. The Prague Spring confirmed to the KGB chief Yuri Andropov that political subversion organised by the west represented the greatest threat to the Soviet Bloc. As a Kremlin confidant, Mielke 'marched in step with the KGB in its efforts to defeat dissidence'. His strategy on dissidence was essentially that advocated by Andropov in that surveillance was used as a tool to detect unwelcome developments before they fully manifested themselves.

Stasi expansion reflected changes in society following the so-called 'Summer of Love' in 1967. Young people in both the East and West were developing a political consciousness as a result of expanded university education, the underground press, radical literature, and trends in popular culture. Those holding the levers of power were no longer quite so certain of themselves. Having survived the crises of 1953 and 1961, the Stasi now faced an altogether new challenge. An increasingly educated and politically aware younger population now had the ideological tools to penetrate the myth of the worker's paradise. As Mielke saw it, the answer to this challenge was to strike before political awareness was translated into dissident action. The growth of the Stasi served to facilitate a surveillance operation which encompassed virtually all East German society. During this time, family members spied on each other, workers denounced their colleagues, informants posed as dissidents, honey-trap operations were conducted, dedicated departments spied on the National People's Army and the People's Police, postal and telephone services were monitored, and literary groups and church circles were infiltrated. Never had a nation been subjected to surveillance and repressive measures to such an extent.

In addition to monitoring the activities of the public and state institutions, the Stasi 'facilitated and sometimes even manipulated East German economic, political, and cultural developments'. They also ran a prison system, maintained guards' units, a Stasi academy, medical services, a bank, and numerous sports teams. The size of the Stasi and the extent of its activities raises the important question—was the Stasi a state within a state?

Max Weber said that a state is essentially, 'a human community that successfully claims the monopoly of the legitimate use of physical force within a given territory'. If we accept this definition, then the Stasi was simply just one more organ of the state. Indeed, the subordination of the Stasi to the state was laid down in Article 1 of the Constitution of the Democratic Republic of East Germany in 1968. This article defined the state as, 'the political organisation of workers in the city and on the land under the leadership of the working class and its Marxist–Leninist party'. The following year, a second statute (replacing that of 1953) expressed more fully the subordination of the Stasi to the party.

While the Stasi made every effort to expand its authority, it remained, as historian Siegfried Suckut argued, 'little more than an eager, perhaps over-eager assistant of the party'. Mielke strongly refuted Erich Honecker's assertion that the activities of the security services had contradicted Politburo decrees by adopting a Chekist model. However, historians generally concur that there are no known instances of Mielke trying to subvert the party or its leadership. As a member of the Politburo (although not a full member until 1976), Mielke had some say on policy making, however his influence was 'institutionalised within party channels'. Moreover, many of the issues that concerned the Stasi were not discussed formally, but were talked about in confidence during one-to-one meetings with Honecker after the weekly Politburo meeting. This form of contact suited Mielke as he was deeply suspicious of Honecker's inner circle. While no records exist of these meetings, it appears that Mielke readily accepted that his ministry was the 'sword and shield' of the party. Mielke certainly used his privileged access to Honecker to extract the maximum resources for his organisation. However, as this did not present any problems as long as they 'operated on a broad consensus on means and ends'. Therefore, as a result of this consensus, the Stasi continued to grow exponentially.

The prolific growth of the Stasi can largely be attributed to breaking with the established practice of recruiting security agents from the aristocracy and the intelligentsia. The Stasi recruited from the working class, some of whom were veteran Communists. This egalitarian approach to recruitment offered considerable opportunities for career advancement to those with energy and commitment. Indeed, political reliability and commitment to the cause was prized above intellectual ability. This practice ensured that the Stasi 'never became a hotbed of reform'. However, it was also counterproductive in that many Stasi employees were 'uneducated and initially, at least, quite incompetent'. The idea of the Stasi as a surprisingly inefficient, ineffective organisation has gained much ground in recent years.

The memoirs of former Stasi operative Manfred Bols cast some light on the frustrations experienced in working for an impotent colossus. Bols joined the Stasi in 1966, not out of political conviction, but for personal gain. Unlike many of his colleagues, Bols was from a middle-class background and was university educated. As a well-educated Stasi officer, he could certainly look forward to swift promotion, and commensurate financial remuneration. Within six months, he would also be eligible for a two-room apartment with a kitchen and a bath. Many Stasi officers had personal weaknesses which affected their efficiency. Bols was no exception, in that his opportunism and careerism meant that his main focus was to stay on the Stasi gravy train as long as possible. As an officer in the Department of Enlightenment, Bols was tasked with developing espionage operations in West Germany. Enormous effort was put into these operations, but they seldom bore fruit as 'agents inadvertently blew their alibis, informants suffered from personal weaknesses, targeted individuals were poorly chosen, and so on'. This catalogue of failure not only summed up Stasi operations in Europe, but in other Cold War theatres of operations too.

During the early 1980s, Bols was stationed in Tanzania. During this time he failed to infiltrate the West German embassy in Dar es Salaam, failed to recruit reliable informants, and failed to develop any meaningful contacts with revolutionary movements. Following his recall to East Germany, Bols experienced the collapse of Communism. In his memoir he stated that 'between September and December 1989 we waited passively in our offices for decisions of the party and state leadership, for guidelines and orders'. Failure upon failure, a pointless task in Tanzania and the stupefaction of the Stasi and party leadership all pointed to Bols having wasted twenty-three years of his life in a ruthless, repressive, but largely ineffective organisation.

If the Stasi was a largely ineffective organisation, does it then follow that its long-serving leader Erich Mielke was a poor leader? During his 1993 trial for the murder of a Berlin policeman in 1931, the presiding judge Theodor Seidel described Mielke as 'one of the most fearsome dictators and police ministers in the 20th century'. While Mielke was no intellectual, he possessed enough intelligence, diligence, thoroughness, ruthlessness, and attention to detail to lead a huge security organisation. His junior staff were kept under strict discipline, and any operative who infringed his ministry's strict code of secrecy was severely punished. However, Mielke was no unthinking brute; he was a man of unscrupulous cunning and mendacity.

Mielke was born into poverty in Berlin's working-class district of Wedding in 1907. His parents were founding members of the German Communist Party in 1918. Mielke joined the youth wing of the party three years later. In 1927, he became a full member of the party, participating in the organisational and propaganda activities of the self-help group Red Aid, the agitprop group Red Wedding, the newspaper *Red Flag*, and the self-protection unit which fought the National Socialists in vicious street battles. The Berlin police were also regarded by the Communist leadership as an enemy. Most hated of all was Captain Paul Anlauf who regularly led police detachments in violently breaking up illegal Communist meetings. On the urging of regional party leader Walter Ulbricht, Anlauf was to be targeted for assassination. Mielke and fellow Communist Erich Ziemer were selected for the task.

On the evening of 9 August 1931, Anlauf, Sergeant Willig, and Captain Franz Lenck were lured to the Babylon Cinema situated on the corner of Bülowplatz and Kaiser-Wilhelm-Straße. As they reached the door, Mielke and Ziemer opened fire at point-blank range. Lenck was hit in the chest and died on the steps of the cinema. Anlauf was hit twice in the neck and died in the arms of Sergeant Willig who had himself been hit in the left arm and his stomach. Following the successful assassination, Mielke was whisked off to Leningrad and then Moscow by agents of the Comintern. In Moscow he attended the International Lenin School under the alias of Paul Bach.

After graduating from the Lenin School, Mielke served with the International Brigade in Spain under the alias of Fritz Leissner. During this time, he served in El Servicio de Información Militar (Military Security Service). While the organisation was nominally controlled by Spanish

Communists, Mielke took his orders from General Alexander Orlov. His main task was weeding out 'deviationists' from among the International Brigade's own ranks. In the winter of 1936, Mielke (in the guise of Captain Leissner) arrested a German company commander named Walter Janka. This former exile and writer came under suspicion because he had made his way to Spain independently. Mielke interrogated him harshly, demanding to know what he was doing in Spain. Janka defiantly held out, giving as good as he got. After a few weeks, Mielke's patience ran out, but rather than liquidating his victim, he demoted him to private. Mielke personally escorted Janka to a new frontline unit. Janka later spoke bitterly about his experience stating that, 'While I was fighting at the front, Mielke served in the rear, shooting Trotskyists and anarchists'. According to Bernd Kaufmann, the former director of the Stasi espionage school, 'The Soviets trusted Mielke implicitly. He earned his spurs in Spain'. Perhaps we will never know how many were tortured, imprisoned, and executed in order for Mielke to win his spurs, but by the end of the Civil War it probably ran into hundreds, if not thousands.

In April 1939, Mielke fled across the Pyrenees to France where he was interned with thousands of other members of the International Brigade. He was still in the internment camp at the outbreak of war in September 1939. What happened for the next six years remains veiled in a carefully woven cloak of lies and obfuscations created by Mielke. It is known that after the war he made his own way to Berlin, where on 15 July 1945, he offered his services to the German Communists. On his party application, Mielke stated that after being released from internment, he moved to Belgium where under the cover name of Gaston, he worked for an underground Communist newspaper. He then went on to claim that following his return to France, he was conscripted into the Organisation Todt to work on construction projects. Mielke concluded his application with some details about his time in Moscow that were specifically chosen in order to ingratiate himself with the Soviet military authorities:

> During my stay in the Soviet Union, I participated in all party discussions of the German Communist Party and in the trials against the enemies and traitors of the Soviet Union.... I was a guest on the honour grandstand of Red Square during the May Day and October Revolution parades. I became acquainted with many comrades of the Federation of World Communist Parties and the War Council of the Special Commission of the Comintern. I will never forget my meeting with Comrade Dimitrov, the chairman of the Comintern with whom I served as an aide together with another comrade. I saw Comrade Stalin during all demonstrations at Red Square, especially when I stood on the grandstand. I mention

> these meetings because all these comrades are our models and teachers for our work.

Colonel General Ivan Serov (commander of the Soviet intelligence and security services) accepted Mielke's account without demur. His future in the Soviet zone of occupation was now assured. Towards the end of July, Mielke was installed as the deputy leader of the 5th Commissariat, a shadowy organisation tasked with apprehending Nazis and anti-Communists. Mielke and his colleagues went about their work with such zeal that soon the prisons could no longer cope. Serov therefore established a system of Gulags, out of a total of thirteen; two were former Nazi concentration camps. Buchenwald became Soviet Special Camp No.1, and Sachsenhausen became Soviet Special Camp No.7. Between 1945 and 1950, 160,000 Germans were sent to these Gulags. The conditions were so brutal that 65,000 inmates died. Of the remaining prisoners, 36,000 were transferred to prisons in the Soviet Union, and 46,000 were freed.

Mielke carefully cultivated the leader of the German Communist Party. Within a short time he had managed to become Ulbricht's closest confidant. Ulbricht's patronage ensured that Mielke was appointed as head of the German Economic Commission, an innocuous sounding organisation whose real task was to investigate 'economic crimes'. Mielke focused his considerable energies on developing his own power base by making himself incredibly useful in identifying and punishing enemies of the state. His diligence was duly rewarded by his promotion to deputy head of the Ministry for State Security and by his election to the party's Central Committee.

During the early 1950s, Mielke was particularly active in purging the party of so-called 'enemies of the working class'. He was also complicit in the torture and imprisonment of West German Communists, the kidnapping of several lawyers involved in the documentation of East German legal abuses, and the kidnap, trial, and imprisonment of journalists. Any party functionary who disagreed with the leadership's decisions was declared an enemy of the people. In 1950, Mielke personally interrogated long-standing party member Leo Bauer after luring him to East Berlin with the false promise of a job in the state radio organisation. According to Bauer, Mielke beat him 'worse than a dog'. Eventually Bauer cracked under the pressure and signed a 180-page confession. He was then handed over to a Soviet military tribunal who sentenced him to death. Only Stalin's own death three years later saved Bauer. The imaginative forms of cruelty and violence employed by Mielke were characteristic of his personality as a dedicated Marxist–Leninist, one for whom society was the anvil to be hammered by the organs of state security.

The popular worker's uprising in June 1953 was put down with great ferocity. However, it shook the ruling party to the core. The already insecure leadership became even more anxious when Max Fechner, the Minister of Justice, declared that belonging to a strike council or being a ringleader were not sufficient grounds for arrest and conviction. Mielke had Fechner arrested as an 'enemy of the state and the party'. He was remanded in custody at the Berlin-Hohenschönhausen Prison before being sentenced and subsequently transferred to the notorious Bautzen Prison, known by its inmates as the 'Yellow Misery' on account of the building's yellow walls. Fechner was replaced by East Germany's hanging judge Hilde Benjamin, whose political fanaticism and harsh verdicts earned her the sobriquets 'Bloody Hilde', 'The Red Freisler', and 'The Red Guillotine'.

Mielke then used the uncertainty plaguing the party as a pretext for a coup against his own chief. He convinced a party commission that state security minister Wilhelm Zaisser was responsible for letting the worker's uprising get out of hand. He also accused Zaisser of plotting his own coup against the party leadership and of wanting to seek a rapprochement with the West. The party sided with Mielke. Zaisser was removed from his post, expelled from the Politburo and Central Committee, and stripped of his party membership. What Mielke did not anticipate was that the party leadership had already decided to subordinate the Stasi to the Ministry of the Interior. Ernst Wollweber was named as state secretary, while Mielke had to be content with the post of deputy. For four years Wollweber and Mielke worked closely together, scoring notable successes against the American intelligence services. In 1955, the Stasi's efforts were rewarded with a restoration to full ministry status. Meanwhile, Wollweber remained blissfully unaware that his seemingly loyal subordinate was biding his time. Only when the time was right would Mielke launch another coup to further his own ambitions.

Success in the intelligence field was one thing, but East Germany still lacked legitimacy and popular support. As such, the regime was susceptible to the challenges of West Germany's society, economy, and state. These challenges produced an atmosphere of intense insecurity amongst the Communist leadership which suited Mielke's book. Wollweber's emphasis on foreign intelligence operations rankled with Ulbricht who was far more focused on keeping the East German population in check. Wollweber was also known to be close to Politburo member Karl Schirdewan, an outspoken reformer who was highly critical of Ulbricht's repressive policies. On 1 November 1957, Wollweber resigned from his post, ostensibly on grounds of ill health. Mielke stepped into his shoes the very same day.

Ever distrustful of reform, Ulbricht readily acquiesced to Stasi demands for greater surveillance and repression. While the capable

Markus Wolf concentrated on foreign intelligence, Mielke focused on stemming the haemorrhage of valuable East German workers seeking sanctuary in the West, forcing the collectivisation of farms, enforcing the 'Right to Work Law' which effectively outlawed strikes, and rooting out disgruntled officials.

Ulbricht's feeling of insecurity was exacerbated by the burgeoning West German economy which served as a magnet for his own dissatisfied and downtrodden workforce. As the tide threatened to turn into a flood, Ulbricht took radical action by turning East Berlin into a prison. The fact that the whole population was taken entirely by surprise on 'Barbed Wire Sunday' was totally attributable to Mielke who enforced a strict code of silence amongst his own staff, the People's Police, and the National People's Army.

By 1970, Ulbricht had recognised that his economically enfeebled state needed propping up if it was to survive in any form. With little economic and material support coming from Moscow, he turned to the West. The West German chancellor's new *Ostpolitik* encouraged him to imagine that a confederation with the more economically powerful West Germany was a possibility. In the Kremlin, alarm bells began to sound as Ulbricht's increasing unilateralism was giving cause for concern. The Soviet first deputy Alexei Kosygin personally warned him that, Brandt's policies, like those of NATO, were 'aimed at the entire Socialist camp'. Ulbricht chose to ignore Kosygin, arguing that strengthened trade relations with West Germany were a vital component in the survival of his regime. Ulbricht's increasingly unmanageable behaviour stretched Moscow's patience to breaking point. The time had come to replace him with someone more malleable. As far as the Communist Party general secretary Leonid Brezhnev was concerned, Ulbricht would be no loss. For some time, he had harboured an intense dislike for the East German leader's 'superior attitude' and arrogant, independent style.

The Soviet leadership chose Erich Honecker as Ulbricht's successor. At a meeting in Moscow, he was urged to take the initiative in removing the obstreperous leader, Brezhnev reassuring him that, 'We will react to any moves on Walter's part regarding unity of leadership and the party. I tell you very openly that it will not be possible to undertake any moves against you and other comrades of the Politburo. After all, we have our troops there with you'. Honecker knew that he not only needed the support of the Soviet leadership, but the support of the East German security services too. On his return to Berlin, he wasted no time in initiating Mielke into the planned coup.

Mielke went on to play a pivotal role in the coup by successfully isolating Ulbricht from his supporters in the Politburo. Following a series of public spats with Honecker, Ulbricht was determined to stamp his authority on the party at the planned meeting of the Sixteenth Plenary Session of the Central Committee on 3 May 1971. However, Mielke had already taken steps to ensure that the hubristic leader's most die-hard supporters would be denied access to the meeting hall. Mielke also infiltrated Ulbricht's own security detail, replacing two of his regular bodyguards with hand-picked men. These men successfully kept an unsuspecting Ulbricht occupied until the session was all but over, and Honecker had been elected as Secretary General of the party, first secretary of the Central Committee, and chairman of the National Defence Council. By way of compensation, Ulbricht was given the chairmanship of the State Council of East Germany. Previously this role carried with it considerable power, however it was now reduced to an entirely ceremonial role.

The ousting of Ulbricht boosted Mielke's career significantly. He benefited materially too, particularly following his move into the party elite's housing compound at Wandlitz. Here, the staunch Socialist enjoyed hunting, saunas, the best food and drink, and around-the-clock maid service. In 1976, his career reached its zenith following his admittance to the Politburo as a full member. With the influence that Politburo status carried, he was able to greatly expand his organisation with 'an absurdly huge network' of informers. These informers were the eyes and ears of a repressive state organisation which had inherited the Soviet model of using violence in the service of the party. Mielke's policy of 'preventive security' essentially served both the state's interests and his own. In essence, he was a master of opportunism and self-preservation who preached water while drinking wine.

The legacy of the organisation he ran for so long is one of moral corruption. The Stasi may not have produced a mountain of corpses like the Gestapo and the SS, but it toyed with the lives of the East German population, turning brother against brother, and father against daughter. The apparent omnipresence of Stasi agents and informers 'provided the regime with its *arcana imperii,* the power of mystification and secrecy on which its capacity to corrupt independent action, stifle dissent, and preclude the emergence of a public realm depended'. Accordingly, individuals modified their behaviour, sometimes to the extent of betraying their friends or family members. More than anything, the record of personal betrayal contained within the Stasi files has come to characterise the repressive East German regime. That legacy endures, and still today there are families whose wounds will never heal, and victims who are so damaged by their experiences that they can never feel secure again.

16

Lichtenberg-Hohenschönhausen Viewpoints

Viewpoint (D1): Stasi Headquarters Museum (Ruschestrasse, 103, House 1, Berlin)

The Stasi Museum is located in House 1 of the former headquarters of the Ministry for State Security. In January 1990, a round table of representatives of the Socialist Unity Party of Germany and civil rights groups agreed that a 'memorial and research centre for DDR Stalinism' should be set up. However, nothing concrete came of this agreement, and so the Berlin Citizen's Committee and various civil rights groups took on the project. On 7 November 1990, the 'Normannenstraße Research and Memorial Site' opened with the exhibition 'Against the Sleep of Reason'.

Since 1990, the 'Anti-Stalinism Action' group have shown changing exhibitions focusing on providing information about the State Security organisation and how its operations impacted upon the population of East Germany. In January 2015, a new permanent exhibition was created in cooperation with the Stasi Records Agency. The exhibition, 'State Security in the SED Dictatorship' looks at the structure, development and operations of the Ministry of State Security. It also provides fascinating insights into 'the people who worked for this institution and the methods they employed'. The exhibition is presented over three floors of the building. The whole second floor consists of Mielke's offices which are preserved in their original state.

Open Monday–Friday 10:00 hrs–18:00 hrs and Saturday–Sunday 11:00 hrs–18:00 hrs.

Guided tours in English are available Thursday–Monday. These tours start at 15:00 hrs (no booking required)

Tel. 0049 30 553 6854

Web: info@stasimuseum.de

The Stasi Museum.

Stasi Museum exhibition.

Viewpoint (D2): Berlin-Hohenschönhausen Memorial (Genslerstrasse, 66, Berlin)

In June 1945, the NKVD (Soviet secret police) converted a former National Socialist People's Welfare Organisation facility into a detention and transit camp which came to be known as Soviet Special Camp No.3. Over a period of just under a year-and-a-half, an estimated 20,000 prisoners passed through the camp on their way to other Gulags in Germany and the Soviet Union. Among them was the German actor Heinrich George who first made his name in the films *Lady Hamilton* (1921) and *Metropolis* (1926) and *Orient Express* (1927). A Communist by conviction, George nevertheless managed an accommodation with the Nazi's who later came to regard him as an actor of note. During the National Socialist period, George played a supporting role in the nauseating propaganda film *Jew Suß* (1940), and the epic colour film *Kolberg* (1945). George was transferred to Sachsenhausen where he subsequently succumbed to starvation in September 1946. In all, some 3,000 prisoners are thought to have perished at the Hohenschönhausen camp between June 1945 and October 1946. Their bodies were dumped in Berlin's many bomb craters. Most lay undiscovered for years.

Following the final transfer of prisoners from the camp in September 1946, the site lay dormant until it was taken over by the Stasi in 1951. During the late 1950s slave labourers added a new prison building to the existing site. After the construction of the Berlin Wall, the prison was mainly used to detain those who wished to leave or those had had actually attempted to escape. Physical torture of prisoners was rare, but psychological torture was employed on a regular basis to break individual prisoner's will. Typical methods employed at the time included sensory deprivation, sleep deprivation, and threats to family and friends. Following the closure of the prison in 1989, it was subsequently granted status as a historical site in 1992.

The historical site can only be visited as part of a guided tour. English speaking tours for up to six people run daily between 11:30 hrs–14:30 hrs. For groups of seven or more, contact the museum on their website in order to register your visit.
Tel. 0049 30 986082 -30
Web: www.stiftung-hsh.de

The Stasi Prison Memorial Site. (*Wikimedia Commons*)

17

Radical Consciousness and the New Sensibility—Rudi Dutschke

The Free University in Berlin had been established at the height of the airlift as a countermeasure to the increasingly politicised institutions being created in the Soviet zone. Accordingly, the constitution of the university was the most liberal in the whole of West Germany. The so-called 'Berlin Model' allowed for student representation at Faculty level, as well as on the academic Senate. Theoretically at least, the constitution provided the basis for a democratic system in which all sections of the academic community could come together in order to debate current issues. However, the expansion of university education during the 1950s and 1960s led to the creation of large, impersonal institutions in which both students and junior staff felt increasingly frustrated by their lack of representation. In 1958, the author and historian Erich Kuby gave a speech at the Free University in which he commented on how 'unfree' the institution really was. He subsequently received a ban from speaking again at the university from both the Rector Hubert Lüers and the Senate. The ban elicited a storm of protest from students, who on following the lead of the University of California's 'Free Speech Movement' claimed that their own university's constitution was being violated. Their strident demands for the right to hear anyone speak on any subject marked the beginnings of the student protest movement.

Until the mid-1960s, student protest was largely focused on issues such as university reform. However, the new sensibility which developed in the wake of the American administration's involvement in Vietnam created a 'desire to use issues like university reform as a springboard from which to launch an attack upon capitalist society'. The sociologist and philosopher Michael Löwy described the motivation of student protestors at this time as a type of 'revolutionary romanticism, a protest against the foundations of modern industrialist/capitalist civilisation, its productivism, and its consumerism, and a unique combination of subjectivity, desire and utopia'. For the Marxist theorist Herbert Marcuse, the revolutionary student movement offered Germany a means to come to terms with its past by creating an aesthetic ethos in which the productive-creative process operated in an atmosphere of freedom. When he spoke of freedom, Marcuse was referring to the elimination of guilt in a war-burdened post-war generation. In his book *An Essay on Liberation,* Marcuse expounded on the conflict between students, the Nazi generation, and the complacency of bourgeois German society:

> The new sensibility, which expresses the ascent of the life instincts over aggressiveness and guilt, would foster, on a social scale, the vital need for the abolition of injustice and misery.... This would be the sensibility of men and women who do not have to be ashamed of themselves anymore because they have overcome their sense of guilt: they have learned not to identify themselves with the false fathers who have built and tolerated and forgotten the Auschwitzs and Vietnams of history, the torture chambers of all the secular and ecclesiastical inquisitions and interrogations, the ghettos and the monumental temples of the corporations, and who have worshipped the higher culture of this reality. If and when men and women break free from this identification, they will have broken the chain which linked the fathers and the sons from generation to generation. They will not have redeemed the crimes against humanity, but they will have become free to stop them and to prevent their recommencement.... The new sensibility has become, by this very token, *praxis*: it emerges in the struggle against violence and exploitation where this struggle is waged for essentially new ways and forms of life: negation of the entire Establishment, its morality, culture; affirmation of the right to build a society in which the abolition of poverty and toil terminates in a universe where the sensuous, the playful, the calm, and the beautiful become forms of existence and thereby the *Form* of the society itself.

The Platonic utopia envisioned by Marcuse could only be created by a liberated social consciousness. As he saw it, the historic task of the student body was to free themselves from a university structure which existed solely to serve the needs of industry 'through the provision of unthinking technocrats or non-political cogs in the capitalist machine who were unable to look beyond the premises upon which the Federal Republic was founded'. From late 1965, the Liberal Student Federation of Germany began to direct its activities towards attacking the thin veneer of democratic representation at Berlin's Free University to expose what they regarded as the Fascist reality lurking beneath.

On 28 January 1966, a small bomb detonated at the Berlin Technical University during a discussion on the Vietnam War. There was very little damage and no casualties, but the message was clear, violent protest was now an acceptable weapon in the struggle against the capitalist hegemony. Three days later, the Free University received an anonymous bomb threat. In response, the university declared a ban on the use of meeting rooms for political discussions. The inevitable storm of protest followed, leading to an ever-deepening pool of mistrust developing between the student body and the university authorities.

A new crisis developed the following month following a decision made by the university authorities to limit student's duration of study in order to alleviate severe overcrowding. By late 1965, the Free University had more than 15,000 students, 5,000 more than was originally intended. On 14 February 1966, the Faculty of Law became the first department to implement these new restrictions by limiting students to nine semesters, after which they would have to leave the university. In May, the Faculty of Medicine followed suit. The student representative body called for a referendum on the issue. On 20 June, student representative Knut Nevermann's request for meeting room in which to hold the referendum was formally denied. Nevermann later recalled how this issue became the starting point for a concerted student protest movement:

> A major issue was the expulsion of students, as we called it. Completely unexpectedly for us, the university administration decided that student registration should be time limited—for a standard period of study days plus two semesters, as we would describe it today. We were extremely angry about that. What also drove us to rebel was the geopolitical event, the Vietnam War. In February 1966, thousands demonstrated in Berlin against the war. Eggs were thrown at the Amerika-Haus on Hardenbergstraße, which was a huge provocation. After all, we were sincerely grateful to the Americans for allowing us to live in freedom.

On 22 June, the student anger described by Nevermann manifested itself in the first ever organised sit-in at a German university. This sit-in was also notable for being the first occasion during which student leader Rudi Dutschke elucidated his anti-authoritarian theories in public. Over the next two years, his speeches would provide the clarion call which galvanised students into taking to the streets in order to demand social change.

While on the surface the sit-in at the Free University appeared to be a spontaneous gesture, it was in reality a well-thought-out and executed example

Rudi Dutschke (in leather jacket) leading a demonstration in Berlin.

of the new student manipulation and provocation tactics designed by student leaders such as Dutschke. Marcuse provided some valuable insights into the rationale behind this student sit-in by expounding on the doctrine of protest:

> If now, in the rebellion of the young intelligentsia, the right and the truth of the imagination become the demands of political action, if surrealistic forms of protest and refusal spread throughout the movement, this apparently insignificant development may indicate a fundamental change in the situation. The political protest, assuming a total character, reaches a dimension which, as aesthetic dimension, has been essentially apolitical. And the political protest activates in this dimension precisely the foundational, organic elements—the human sensibility which rebels against the dictates of repressive reason, and, in doing so, invokes the sensuous power of the imagination. The political action which insists on a new morality and a new sensibility as preconditions and results of social change occurs at a point at which the repressive rationality that has brought about the achievements of industrial society becomes utterly regressive—rational only in its efficiency to 'contain' liberation. Beyond the limits (and beyond the power) of repressive reason now appears the prospect for a new relationship between sensibility and reason, namely, the harmony between sensibility and a radical consciousness.

In essence, Marcuse was saying that students had developed a sensitivity to the authoritarian structures which dominated their lives, and that freedom from these structures could be attained by liberating their aesthetic impulses in order to create a radical consciousness.

The radical consciousness emerging from the new sensibility found expression in the alternative lifestyle choices of Commune 1. The 'patriarch' of the communards was Dieter Kunzelman, an associate of Dutschke in the anti-authoritarian wing of the student representative body. Under Kunzelman's leadership, the commune adopted the style of the Situationists and the American Yippies by combining political activity with satirical provocation. The main focus of communard activity was Vietnam. On 6 April 1967, students from the Free University planned a demonstration against the war during a visit to the capital by American Vice-President Hubert Humphrey. Commune 1 also planned a stunt involving the throwing of smoke bombs and blancmange filled bags to coincide with the student protest. Having got wind of the plan, the police raided the commune. Convinced that this was a genuine assassination attempt, details of the dastardly plot were released to the press before the facts were fully known. The bias of the police was eclipsed by the conservative press, who with complete certainty trumpeted the news of the attempted assassination. The next day, both *Bild* and the *Berliner Morgenpost* were forced to admit that the reported assassination attempt was a fantasy. Neither the police nor the conservative press would ever forgive or forget their humiliation at the hands of these political pranksters.

With tensions rising between those in authority and those wishing to dismantle authoritative structures, it was only a matter of time before violence exploded onto the streets. The catalyst for violence was the impending state visit of the Shah of Persia. Students at the Free University openly accused the Shah of being a corrupt despot, accusations repeated by Ulrike Meinhof who penned an open letter to the Shah's wife in the monthly left-wing *Konkret* magazine. On 1 June, a debate was held at the Free University during which Dr Bahman Nirumand, a noted critic of the Shah, spoke out against his despotic regime. Placards were prepared for the following day's demonstration, along with copious supplies of eggs and tomatoes to throw at the police.

Meanwhile, the police had been given instructions by the Ministry of the Interior to avoid direct confrontation with demonstrators, unless there was an obvious threat to the Shah's security. In theory this 'light-touch' approach would ensure that the Shah's visit to the Schöneberg Town Hall passed off peacefully. However, no plan survives first contact with the opposing forces. In this case, the 'friction' upsetting the plan came in the form of approximately 100 Iranians who had positioned themselves between the police and the demonstrators. These supporters of the Shah were in reality members of the feared Iranian secret service organisation known as Savak. The Iranians got into heated verbal exchanges with demonstrators. Then, a group of between fifteen and twenty of them attacked the demonstrators with long wooden poles. Meanwhile, the police did nothing, as they were effectively paralysed by their orders to concentrate on watching the demonstrators. After the Shah left for his tour of the city, the demonstrators melted away, many moving on to take up new positions for the next round of the contest.

At approximately 18:30 hrs that evening, a large crowd of demonstrators gathered outside of the Opera House where the Shah and his wife were scheduled to watch a performance of *The Magic Flute*. The police erected barriers along Bismarck Straße and Krumme Straße. While in the centre of the road, police lined up facing the demonstrators. At 19:20 hrs the Savak contingent arrived. However, this time the police made at least some attempt to keep them apart from the demonstrators. As eggs, tomatoes, and other missiles flew through the air, the police waded into the demonstrators, dragging several who were suspected of throwing missiles with them. The demonstrators responded with shouts of 'SA, SS' and 'Gestapo'. By 20:00 hrs the demonstration had descended into a what eye witness Heinz-Dieter Kretzmer described as 'a violent hand-to-hand fight'.

Some demonstrators managed to break free, but soon found themselves cornered again, this time in a car park located on the ground floor of an apartment block on the junction of Krumme Straße and Schiller Straße. The police then mounted a 'clearing action' to force the demonstrators from the car park. Another violent confrontation ensued in which the outnumbered demonstrators were forced to give ground. By 20:30 hrs the police had more or less cleared the area. It was then that a shot rang out. Benno Ohnesorg, a twenty-six-year-old literature student from the Free University collapsed to the ground after being shot in the head by plain-clothes officer Karl-Heinz Kurras. The entire scene was witnessed by eight-year-old Hans Bromosch who was leaning out of his parent's ground floor window. Many years later, he recalled the incident in a newspaper interview, stating that, 'He stood there for a long while, and it was when he went to leave that it happened. That was the moment when I saw the person with the pistol. He was standing alone, with no one in the vicinity who could have threatened him'. The eye witness testimony provided by Bromosch at the Moabit District Court hearing in November 1967 was ignored on account of his age. Kurras was subsequently acquitted of negligent manslaughter. The shooting of Ohnesorg, the acquittal of Kurras, and the brutality of the police all served to convince Berlin's radical left that West Germany was on the slippery slope towards authoritarianism.

Ohnesorg's killing together with the ongoing issue of university reform served to escalate tensions between the increasingly politicised student body and the authorities. On 15 October, Professor Ewald Harndt was appointed rector of the Free University. His tenure was characterised by an increasingly vicious conflict, particularly during the first months of 1968. On 26 January 1968, students at the Department of Romance Studies demanded the creation of a Working Committee to reassess the 'premises and methods and the social function' of their department. Their peaceful protest was hijacked by radical students who attempted to smash their way into the room hosting the faculty meeting. The ensuing violence was condemned by the university authorities as being 'inconsistent with rational discussion and argument'. The action of the radical students was widely condemned. Many people in the wider German society now began to regard the student protestors not as romantic revolutionaries, but as a nuisance and a danger.

In East Berlin, the activities of radical students were being monitored and recorded in a secret file entitled 'Youth Protest and Resistance'. This file, for the eyes of Politburo members only, pointed towards the establishment of links with the radical student body:

> Now is the time to focus on the resistance already existent among youths and students in West Germany and West Berlin towards West German government policy, to focus on their demands for a change in policy and the actions carried out by the progressive energies in the various youth and student groups, and to develop these into a unified, steered youth movement in West Germany and West Berlin.... In its character and aims, this movement should be anti-fascistic, anti-militaristic, anti-monopolistic and democratic.

The reference to a 'steered movement' was telling. Notwithstanding, a series of exploratory talks were held between radical student leaders and representatives of the Free German Youth movement. Apart from a few exchanges of information about policemen who were former Nazis, their collaboration came to nothing.

For Dutschke, the silver-tongued spokesperson of the radical left, the repressive policies of the East German regime were diametrically opposed to the new sensibility. His utopian vision could not be contained within the Marxist–Leninist dialectic. For him, the engine of history could be manipulated in order to create a better world. In a 1967 speech, he encouraged his supporters to break free from the straitjacket of history:

> We can change. We are not desperate idiots of history, unable to take their own destiny in their own hands.... Many historical signs indicate

> that history is not an eternal cycle where only the negative must triumph. Why should we renounce this historical possibility and say: we give up, we cannot make it, sometime this world will come to an end. Exactly the opposite. We can construct a world as humanity has never seen before; a world that will distinguish itself for the absence of war and hunger. And this is the whole globe. This is our historical possibility, and should we let it go? I'm not a professional politician, but we are men who do not want the world to continue in this way, and for this reason we will fight, indeed we have already started to fight.

Dutschke's fight was not aimed at the Kafkaesque police states in Eastern Europe as society was trapped within the regime's own internal logic. In trans-historical terms, the imperfect western democracies offered more fertile ground for the facilitation of social change.

Dutschke's call for 'continuous revolt' made him the bogeyman of the West German conservative press. The Springer Press tabloids *Bild-Zeitung* and *Bild am Sonntag* were particularly venomous with regard to their coverage of student protests. While the conservative press as a whole was deeply biased against student activists and demonstrators, the Springer Press was imbued with a loathing for the politics and alternative lifestyles advocated by the likes of Dutschke. Essayist Andreas Juhnke later wrote that Dutschke developed 'a charisma that made him the symbol of the protest and youth movements of the time and also an object of hatred for narrow-minded rightists'. While it is difficult to estimate the extent to which articles in the Springer Press influenced popular anti-radicalism, there can be little doubt that Dutschke was the main target of the conservative press. For Axel Springer, Dutschke represented the Communist threat within.

On the morning of 11 April, Dutschke was asked whether he felt afraid of being attacked on the street. He replied by saying, 'No, fear, no. It may happen, but friends keep an eye on me. Normally I don't walk around on my own'. However, later that day he would venture out alone to a chemist shop on the Kufürstendamm in order to pick up some medicine for his young son Hosea Che. That afternoon, Dutschke was approached by a low skilled painter and labourer from Munich named Josef Bachmann. During the morning, Bachmann had travelled to West Berlin with the express intention of killing the student leader after reading a series of unambiguous articles in *Bild* such as, 'Stop Rudi Dutschke' and 'Stop the terror of the young reds now!'. Before firing three bullets into Dutschke's head, neck, and chest, Bachmann was heard to shout, 'You dirty Communist pig!' Although seriously wounded, Dutschke went on to make a partial recovery. While Bachmann was already known to have strong

The Vietnam Solidarity Congress held at the Berlin Free University *c.* 1968

anti-Communist leanings, the extent to which he had been influenced by the Springer Press only became absolutely clear during his trial.

While giving evidence on the stand, Bachmann confirmed his links with the Springer Press by stating that, ‘I have taken my daily information from the *Bild-Zeitung* and felt that *Bild-Zeitung* reflected not just my views, but also what the masses think. Very many are of my opinion. Or more correctly: I am of their opinion’. Of course, none of this came as a revelation to Dutschke’s supporters. They had long known that the Springer Press had ‘systematically incited the people against the students’. The attempted assassination of the charismatic student leader provoked four days of the worst rioting seen in West Berlin, as thousands of angry students fought running battles with the police, while torching cars and petrol bombing shops.

During the first quarter of 1968, the radical students and the fiery press baron Axel Springer were caught up in a dialectic in which both parties fed off the other’s rhetoric. It was therefore only a matter of time before their conflict came to a head. When more than 2,000 students surrounded the Springer Press headquarters on Berlin’s Kochstraße shouting ‘Springer murderers’ and ‘Springer burn’, the conflict took on a whole new dimension. The building was briefly occupied by the student protestors. Later that evening, Molotov cocktails transformed the car park into a sea of flame. Stuart Hilwig described the scene in *1968: The World Transformed* when he wrote, 'When students surrounded the Springer Press offices, delivery drivers drove through a police gauntlet of barbed wire and braved a barrage of stones and Molotov cocktails to make their daily runs'. Five delivery trucks belonging to the Springer press were destroyed during this night of carnage. However, this was only the beginning.

Over the following days, the so-called 'Easter Riots' took on a new intensity. On the Kurfürstendamm, police units on horseback battled with student protesters. With some justification, *Bild* described the scene as 'a battlefield'. More than 180 protesters were arrested, amongst them was Peter Brandt, son of foreign minister Willy Brandt. Elsewhere, more than 45,000 protesters attempted to storm Springer Press offices in more than twenty cities including Cologne, Essen, Frankfurt, and Munich. The Federal Government responded by ratifying a series of highly controversial emergency laws which came into effect on 28 June 1968.

For many students, the emergency laws came as a harsh blow. With their utopian dreams shattered, they returned to their studies. Meanwhile, others turned to more direct action. Student activist Knut Nevermann later recalled the split in the student movement:

> The protests on Easter Monday were a high point in the student movement, at the same time, the beginning of its end. In November, there

Protesters on the Kurfürstendamm during the violent spring of 1968

> was a fight on Tegeler Weg with many people injured, many more on the side of the police than on the side of the demonstrators—even though there had not been any provocations by the police. After the wild fights, there was a meeting at the Technical University, where many of those present thought we were in a revolutionary situation—what a delusion! That divided the student body. Many withdrew from the political protests and completed their studies.

Moreover, the elitism of the so-called alternative society led to a great deal of disillusionment. The student protest movement was essentially an intellectual, male, middle-class club in which women were adjuncts, and the working-class lookers-on. While the women's liberation movement was still in its infancy, the 1968 protest movement certainly played a part in accelerating the drive towards gender equality.

Dutschke's legacy has long been debated in the German press. After the shooting he underwent a long and painful rehabilitation process in which he struggled to regain his speech and memory. He was never quite the same political force again, although in 1971, the Conservative government in Britain had him thrown out of the country for alleged subversive political activities. His legacy therefore rests almost entirely on the intense period of radical political activity in West Berlin between 1966–1968. Interviewed in 1993, former radical student colleague Bernd Rabehl recalled Dutschke's impact on the so-called '68ers' by saying that he 'stood for the romantic idea of a better society'. Rabehl then went on to say that, 'He was the perfect combination of a charismatic speaker and a serious intellectual. His death turned him into a 'mythical figure'. Dutschke's death in 1979 from a seizure was almost certainly related to the injuries he had received eleven years earlier. Already a martyr, he was then sanctified by death.

Opinion on Dutschke's legacy and that of the whole 1968 student movement remains divided. In a 1993 piece in *Die Zeit,* the prominent political analyst Kurt Sontheimer opined that Dutschke and the 68ers, 'had no interest in fairness or tolerance'. This is perhaps a little unfair, as Dutschke's strategy was not based on instant emancipation, but the slower and surer strategy of the 'long march through the institutions'. In his 1972 pamphlet entitled *Counterrevolution and Revolt,* Marcuse expounded on Dutschke's strategy:

> Rudi Dutschke has proposed the strategy of the long march through the institutions while working within them, but not simply by 'boring from within', rather by 'doing the job', learning how to program and read computers, how to teach at all levels of education, how to use the mass media, how to organise production.

Marcuse understood that the spark which ignited the 1968 student protests owed little to Marxist–Leninist dogma. The students who took to West Berlin's streets were largely of the baby-boom generation who had known nothing but economic growth and the benefits of the burgeoning consumer society. The student movement didn't consist of Communist zealots who were hell-bent on using terror to achieve their ends, but rather, middle-class kids with a utopian dream. As their dream faded towards the end of the 1960s, the naïve pacifism which had characterised their movement was rejected by a new breed of radicals. Amongst them was Horst Mahler who foreshadowed his future career in the Red Army Faction when he stated that, 'We want no agitation with peaceful methods'. Ulrike Meinhof, another future Red Army Faction member said that, 'If one sets one Springer car on fire that is a criminal offence. If one sets a hundred Springer cars on fire; that is political action'. Mahler and Meinhof's questioning of the validity of legal forms of protest inexorably led to a new form of revolt against the state, the urban guerrilla concept.

18

Kreuzberg–Mariendorf Viewpoints

Viewpoint (E1): Kreuzberg: Axel Springer Haus (Axel Springer Strasse, 65, Berlin) & Rudi Dutschke Strasse

Axel Springer Haus—Design and Architectural Features

When publishing magnate Axel Springer decided to build an impressive headquarters in West Berlin, his main aim was to make a symbolic gesture which would characterise the continuity of German culture and traditions in the face of the Soviet threat. Springer's phenomenal publishing success enabled him to wield considerable political power as West Germany's unofficial watchdog and representative. His vision of a democratic (Conservative) Germany which embraced freedom and human rights for all made him a popular figure amongst the wartime generation who yearned for stability. For the 'baby boom' generation he became a figure of hate, symbolising the old conservatism which had helped to usher in Hitler's terror regime. Berlin's radical students regarded Springer's golden skyscraper as the ultimate manifestation of crass consumerism and materialism.

The foundation stone for the new headquarters was laid on 25 May 1959, a mere six months after Khrushchev's notorious 'Berlin Ultimatum'. To even consider such a massive undertaking at this time demonstrates Springer's strong belief in Germany's future. The stunning glass and metal structure designed by architects Melchiorre Bega, Gino Franzi, Franz Heinrich Sobotka, and Gustav Müller also served as the physical manifestation of his political vision. Work on transforming Springer's political vision into reality was accelerated in March 1961, following the demolition of the war-damaged Jerusalem Church. On 28 November 1964, Springer articulated his vision in a speech to his senior employees:

> When we go to Kochstraße, we are not just going to a new, beautiful, large building—not just to the historic newspaper district of Berlin: we are going to represent Germany on Kochstraße. If you don't understand that, if you do not grasp the idea that this is bigger than ourselves, then it is not worth completing the construction of this newspaper house.

The building itself, particularly the nineteenth-floor 'Journalist's Club' was used to promote Springer's vision. Here, receptions for important figures such as the Dalai Lama, George Bush Senior, and Mikhail Gorbachev were hosted in order to pave the way to Germany's eventual reunification.

In more recent years, the grounds around the building have been developed as a home for numerous sculptures and monuments relating to the fall of the Berlin wall and the reunification of Germany. The most prominent sculptures include Stephan Balkenhol's 'Balancing Act' which was unveiled on the fiftieth anniversary of the laying of the building's foundation stone in 2009. The sculpture depicts a man in shirt and trousers balancing on a section of the Berlin Wall. On the night of 17 March 2012, the sculpture was vandalised when red paint was thrown over it. The 'Fathers of the Unity' sculpture by Serge Mangin honours the three key players in German unification, former German Chancellor Helmut Kohl, former American President George Bush Sr., and former President of the Soviet Union Mikhail Gorbachev. The sculpture features three large brass busts, each one bearing a different facial expression. Kohl's bust has what the sculptor described as a 'far sighted serious expression', while that of Gorbachev displays a 'frank leniency'. Most interestingly, Bush's bust shows the former President with 'a paternal grin'.

At the inauguration ceremony on 29 September 2010, the Axel Springer Organisation Chairman praised the fathers of reunification by saying that, 'Kohl had created facts, Gorbachev had deliberately accepted the risk of losing power, and Bush said yes at the right moment'. Former President Ronald Reagan is also honoured on the site with a memorial plaque on to which is inscribed those now famous words, 'Mr Gorbachev, open this gate. Mr Gorbachev, tear down this wall'. While not exactly on the tourist map, the author highly recommends a visit to this site.

Above left: Axel Springer Berlin Headquarters.

Above right: Bronze bust of President George W. Bush.

Rudi Dutschke Straße

In January 2007, a referendum was held in Berlin's Friedrichshain–Kreuzberg district to finally end the controversy surrounding the grass-roots proposal to rename a section of Kochstraße in honour of the 1960s student leader Rudi Dutschke. Peter Unfried, the deputy-editor-in-chief of the left-leaning newspaper *Die Tageszeitung* came out in full support of the proposal:

> Germany and Berlin need a Rudi-Dutschke-Straße, because it's a very important symbol of what we are today and which political stream has made things happen in post-war Germany. What we are today—a freer, more liberal society—is partly due to 1968 and Rudi Dutschke ... It'll be a sort of poetic justice to have Dutschke Boulevard with Axel Springer Street.

The official naming of Rudi Dutschke Straße. (*Wikimedia Commons*)

Following the referendum result which returned a clear 'Yes' vote for the proposal, the Springer Press and the Federal Chamber of Engineers launched a legal challenge. On 21 April 2008, the Upper Berlin–Brandenburg Court rejected the challenge, thus clearing the way for the proposed name change. Commenting on the decision, Dutschke's son Marak said, 'I think it's a positive development. These two streets meeting is a constructive way of dealing with the history between these two opponents from forty years ago'.

The renaming ceremony took place nine days after the defeat of the legal challenge. Interestingly, the renaming of the street was in violation of a district council decision in 2005 to name, or rename streets after females in order to redress the noticeable gender imbalance. Nonetheless, the decision was in this author's view the right one.

Viewpoint (E2): Charlottenburg: Architecture Building (Berlin Institute of Technology) Strasse des 17 Juni, Berlin.

Design and architectural features

The architectural building at Berlin's Technical University was designed in 1966 by architects Bernhard Hermkes and Hans Scharoun. The lower section of the building was designed by Scharoun who was particularly concerned about the interaction between students and their surroundings. The ground floor has an open character, consisting of a foyer and exhibition area. The first floor still largely consists of offices and student workplaces. The second floor was originally designed as a large drawing office, but now serves as the faculty library. The building's exterior, designed by Hermkes displays a considerable amount of concern for student's comfort as the projecting façade panels were suspended at an angle in order to mitigate the effects of direct sunlight.

Scharoun had already achieved much acclaim for his design work on the Berlin Philharmonic Hall which was completed and opened to the public in 1963. This ambitious project features complex interior spaces, complimented by a dynamic exterior fabricated from a golden metal mesh. Hermkes' reputation as a great architect can be traced back to his radical redesign of Ernst-Reuter-Platz which served as a counter-proposal to the prestigious East German housing project on Stalinallee.

The 1968 Student Protest

In May 1968, students protested against the adoption by the Federal Government of the Emergency Acts by occupying the architecture building at the Berlin Technical University. The month of May was the highpoint of the radical left's struggle against a government which they believed was becoming increasingly fascistic. Between 1 May and 29 May, students, workers, and trade unionists came together across the country to form a united front against the reactionary government. Despite the massive scale of the protests, the Bundestag passed the new laws. The failure to achieve radical change through protest led some radicals to view the struggle in terms of an armed conflict. Michael 'Bobbi' Baumann, a founder of the 2 June Movement was an early convert to the idea of armed struggle. The May 1968 protests confirmed that the police, the media, and government bureaucracy could only be challenged by force:

> On the spot, I really got it, this concept of mass struggle terrorism; this problem I had been thinking about for so long became clear to me then. The chance for a revolutionary movement lies in this: when a determined group is there simultaneously with the masses, supporting them through terror.

The left-wing journalist Ulrike Meinhof was thinking along similar lines as it was clear to her that fundamental social change could only be achieved through 'class war'. In a *Konkret* article entitled 'From Protest to Resistance' she argued that 'the boundaries between protest and resistance were exceeded'. In this article, she went on to say that:

> The democratisation of state and society are the aims. The fight against the Emergency Laws is one means among others to achieve those aims, which means depriving the dictators in state and society of power. That doesn't work if one only fights against the change from a large to a small prison cell, and forgets to prepare in advance for a break-out.

By the end of the decade, all the necessary conditions were in place for the transition from protest to violent resistance. In the dying days of the 'swinging 60s', hardly a day went by without sit-ins, demonstrations, counter-demonstrations, fire-bombings, court hearings, press vilification, police brutality, recriminations and counter-recriminations amongst the fractured left-wing radicals. It was clear to many radicals that as the decade came to an end, they had failed to paint it black.

19

A Gangster Drama

The failure to achieve meaningful social change by the broad-based left-wing, anti-imperialist, revolutionary collectives coincided with the fragmentation of their movement. In September 1968, the student activist Hans Jürgen Krahl was pelted with tomatoes by female attendees at a conference after he refused to acknowledge the issue of chauvinism within the student movement. While many women remained loyal to the leftist cause, a considerable number began to identify more closely with the feminist movements that had emerged in America and Britain.

The collapse of the Socialist German Students' Federation sped up the fragmentation of the radical left-wing movement. Meanwhile, other groups attempted to fill the void, amongst them the re-established German Communist Party, Maoist parties, Trotskyist organisations, and the rather strange anti-psychiatry group known as The Socialist Patient Collective. In March 1970, the student federation dissolved itself following a particularly chaotic congress in Frankfurt. The Federal Government responded by offering an amnesty to all students charged with less violent offences. This ploy further fragmented the crumbling student movement as many were only too glad to be allowed to resume their studies.

While the majority of those still loyal to the cause remained committed to achieving change by semi-legal activism, a minority were starting to experiment with more violent means of self-expression. The Maoist element in Commune 1 had carried out a series of fire bombings and bank robberies in 1967. However, many of its members had been arrested by the end of the year and were in no position to capitalise on the collapse of the student movement. However, the remnants of the radical commune scene did provide the leadership for the 2 June Movement, whose rhetoric resonated with the anti-authoritarians, anarchists, and independent socialists. Meanwhile, another guerrilla concept was in the making, one more serious, and more theoretically rigorous.

After setting off incendiary devices in Frankfurt department stores in April 1968, the (then unknown) radicals Andreas Baader and Gudrun Ensslin were arrested and subsequently released, pending their appeal, in June 1969. At this time neither Baader nor Ensslin had any clear vision for turning their urban guerrilla concept into reality. As such, they busied themselves instead with establishing contacts with young runaways from state homes. Former Red Army Faction (RAF) member Astrid Proll later recalled:

> When Andreas Baader and Gudrun Ensslin were released from custody they knew exactly what they wanted. Unlike the drugged communards they radiated great clarity and resolve.... Gudrun and Andreas launched a big campaign in Frankfurt against the authoritarian regimes in young offender institutions. We lived with youths who had escaped from closed institutions, joined them in fighting for their rights, and managed to achieve some successes. Ulrike Meinhof, as a committed critical journalist joined us and became friends with Gudrun and Andreas.

By the early part of 1969, Ulrike Meinhof had become totally disillusioned with *Konkret,* which in her view was losing its political edge. She subsequently left the magazine, explaining that the increasing commercialisation of the magazine 'would become part of the counter-revolution, a thing that I cannot gloss over with my co-operation, especially now that it is impossible to change its course'. Over the coming months, Meinhof committed herself to the Marxist–Leninist guerrilla movement following her prison visits to Ensslin. Following her release, their friendship grew stronger. When Baader, Ensslin, and Proll went on the run following their failed court appeal, Meinhof provided shelter on a number of occasions. Her rather dull life as a journalist was suddenly becoming far more exciting.

On 4 April 1970, Baader (using the pseudonym Peter Chotjewitz) was arrested at a police checkpoint in Berlin. Wasting no time, his confederates quickly devised a plan to free him. Using her journalistic credentials, Meinhof applied for permission to do some work with Baader on a project about youth centres, an area in which they both had some previous experience. The credibility of the request led the authorities to reluctantly grant permission for the work to take place at the Social Issues Library in West Berlin's Dahlem district.

On 14 May, Baader was escorted from Moabit Prison to the library by two armed guards. Just after meeting Meinhof in the library, two young women carrying suitcases and a man (hired because of his supposed experience

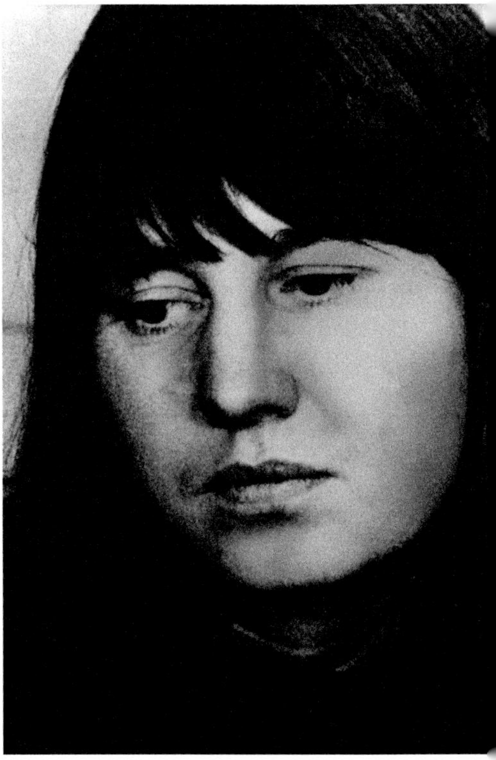

Above left: Andreas Baader.

Above right: Ulrike Meinhof.

Left: Gudrun Ennslin.

with firearms) entered the room where the meeting was taking place. Irene Goergens (a teenager whom Meinhof had met while doing youth work) and Ingrid Schubert (a radical West Berlin doctor) opened the door to allow a masked and armed Ensslin entry, while at the same time producing pistols from their suitcases. When the elderly librarian Georg Linke attempted to intervene, he was shot in the liver by the hired man. Baader and his three female accomplices then made their escape through a window.

For Meinhof, this was the point of no return. Immediately after her escape, she telephoned a friend to pick up her children from school. This action demonstrates that she had no definite plan. The shooting of the librarian changed everything. Astrid Proll, the getaway driver during Baader's escape later explained the impact of the incident on their nascent movement:

> I think we were all very nervous; I remember some people throwing up. Because we weren't so wonderful criminals, we weren't so wonderful with the guns, we sort of involved a so-called criminal who could do it so much better than we, and … He was so nervous that he shot somebody. He didn't kill him, but he shot him very badly, and that was really bad for the whole start of it.… After a man had been severely hurt … we found ourselves on wanted lists. It was an accident that accelerated the underground life of the group. Ulrike Meinhof, who had so far been at the fringes of the group, was all of a sudden wanted on every single bill post for attempted murder against a reward of 10,000 Marks.… When we were underground there were no more discussions, there was only action.

The Baader escape set off such a controversy among the radical left that the group themselves were forced into sending a statement to the radical newspaper *883* in order to fully explain the context of their actions within the class war struggle. The statement was printed at the insistence of cinematography student Holger Meins, who before becoming a future leading figure in the group worked for the newspaper. This first documented statement by the RAF is quoted below *in extensio*:

> Comrades of 883
> It is pointless to explain the right thing to the wrong people. We've done enough of that. We don't want to explain the action to free Baader to babbling intellectuals, to those who are freaked out, to know-it-all's, but rather to the potentially revolutionary section of the people. That is to say, to those who can immediately understand this action, because they are themselves prisoners. Those who want nothing to do with the blather of the 'left' because it remains without meaning or consequence. Those who are fed up!

The action to free Baader must be explained to youth from the Märkisch neighbourhood, to the girls from Eichenhof, Ollenhauer, and Heiligensee, to young people in group homes, in youth centres, in Grünen Haus and Kieferngrund. To large families, to young workers and apprentices, to high school students, to families in the neighbourhoods that are being gentrified, to the workers at Siemens and AEG-Telefunken, at SEL and Osram, to the married women, who, as well as doing the housework and raising the children, must do piecework—damn it.

They are the ones who must understand the action; those who receive no compensation for the exploitation they must suffer... Those who have realised that the future promised to them by their teachers and professors and landlords and social workers and supervisors and foremen and union representatives and city councillors is nothing more than an empty lie, but who nevertheless fear the police. It is necessary that they—and not the petit bourgeois intellectuals—understand that all that is over now, that this is a start, that the liberation of Baader is only the beginning!

...It is to them that we want to say that we are building the red army, and it is their army. It is to them that we say, 'It has begun'... That's why we are building the red army. Behind parents stand the teachers, the youth authorities, and the police. Behind the supervisor stands the boss, the personnel office, the workers compensation board, the welfare office, and the police. With this comes the way that the pigs use censorship, layoffs, dismissals, along with bailiff's seals and billy clubs... They escalate if nothing else does the trick... The pigs will certainly escalate their means as far as possible... To bring this conflict to a head, we are building the red army...

You must understand that those who have nothing to gain from the exploitation of the Third World... have no reason to identify with the exploiter. They can grasp what is beginning to happen here has been going on for a long time in Vietnam, in Palestine, in Guatemala, in Oakland and Watts. In Cuba and China, In Angola and in New York...

Stop lounging around on the sofa in your recently-raided apartment counting up your love affairs and other petty details... Forget about the cowardly shits, the bootlickers, the social workers, those who only attempt to curry favour, they are a lumpen mob. Figure out where the asylums are and the large families and the sub-proletariat and the women workers, those who are only waiting to give a kick in the teeth to those who deserve it. They will take the lead. And don't let yourselves get caught. Learn from them how one avoids getting caught—they know more about it than you.
Develop the class struggle
Organise the proletariat
Start the armed struggle
Build the red army!

A month later, *Der Spiegel* published a statement by Meinhof in which she attempted to justify the freeing of Baader. In a rambling text full of hate filled language such as, 'We say the type in uniform is a pig, he is no human', she only partially succeeded in making clear the RAF's political objectives. More statements were to follow, each so convoluted and theory bound that their meaning was all but lost to the reader.

On 21 June 1970, Baader, Ensslin, Meinhof and several other group members travelled to Jordan where they received guerrilla tactics training by the Palestine Liberation Organisation (PLO). During this time, the group learned how to handle the ubiquitous AK-47 assault rifle, along with the tactics necessary to disrupt an authoritarian regime. However, their training did not always go smoothly, as Baader ruffled quite a few feathers when he expressed the view that much of the training received was irrelevant. As he saw it, the RAF had far more in common with the Uruguayan Tupamaros movement which espoused a similar interpretation of 'class war'. Meanwhile, the PLO were fighting a different kind of war altogether. Nonetheless, Baader was able to make some useful contacts, particularly Ali Hassan Salameh who led the Fatah Force 17 commando and special operations unit, and who later went on to act as Chief of Operations for the Black September group who carried out the 1972 Munich massacre. From time to time, the Middle East would become a convenient spot to lie low when Europe became 'too hot'.

Following their return to West Berlin on 9 August 1970, the RAF set about acquiring funds for their future operations. On 29 September, the group scored a spectacular success when they raided three West Berlin banks simultaneously. A fourth bank was to be hit, but the operation was called-off when it was found to be full of construction workers. These daring raids, in which not a shot was fired, netted the RAF over 200,000 Marks. However, on 8 October the group suffered a serious setback when members Horst Mahler, Ingrid Schubert, Brigitte Asdonk and Monika Berberich were arrested following an anonymous tip which revealed the location of their two West Berlin safe houses. Following these arrests, the group began moving the focus of their operations away from Berlin. In November, the group raided the Munsterlager situated near Lüneburg Heath for weapons. Additional weapons were also acquired at this time through Fatah contacts. During that same month, burglaries at two city halls yield significant quantities of blank identification cards, passports, and official stamps. On 15 January 1971, two banks in Kassel were raided, further increasing the RAF's fighting fund.

On 10 February, the police in Frankfurt-am-Main opened fire on Astrid Proll and Manfred Grashof following a routine identity check. None of the police bullets hit their mark, and as their luck held, the two urban guerrillas made their escape. The evidence (suppressed at the time) shows that neither Proll nor Grashof drew their weapons. However, the alleged 'firefight' provided enough justification for Federal Minister of the Interior, Hans-Dietrich Genscher, to start nationwide searches for the organisation now branded as 'Public Enemy Number One'.

Meanwhile, the imprisoned RAF member Horst Mahler was publishing interviews and 'cell circulars' which were rejected by the rest of the group as theoretically unsound. In response, Meinhof was asked to use her journalistic skills to produce a manifesto that would more accurately reflect the group's ideological underpinnings. The resulting document was the RAF's first real statement of purpose. It drew heavily on Mao, the early Italian autonomist of *il Manifesto*, and the class warfare theories being developed at the time in Latin America. The importance of this document cannot be understated; therefore it will be quoted *in extensio*:

> Some comrades have already made their minds up about us. For them, it is the 'demagoguery of the bourgeois press' that links these 'anarchist groups' with the socialist movement. In their incorrect and pejorative use of the term anarchism, they are no different from the Springer Press. We don't want to engage in dialogue on such a shabby basis.
>
> Many comrades want to know what we think we are doing. The letter to 833, in May 1970, was too vague … Almost everything in the newspapers written about us has been a lie. Plans to kidnap Willie Brandt are meant to make us look like political idiots, and claims that we intend to kidnap children are meant to make us look like unscrupulous criminals. These lies go as far as the 'authentic details' in *Konkret # 5*, which proved to be nothing more than unreliable details that have been slapped together. That we have 'officers and soldiers', that some of us are slaves of others, that comrades who have left us fear reprisals, that we broke into houses or used violence to take passports, that we exercise 'group terror'—all of this is bullshit….
>
> Many comrades spread untruths about us too. They brag that we lived with them, that they organised our trip to Jordan, that they know about our contacts, that they are doing something for us, when, in fact, they are doing nothing. Some only want to make it look like they are 'in the know'…. In reality, they are irrelevant to us…. We want nothing to do with these gossipmongers, for whom the anti-imperialist struggle is a coffee klatch…. Our existence makes some people feel pressured to justify themselves…. For example, the rumour is still circulating that Baader had only three or nine or twelve months to serve, though the correct length of time is easily ascertained: three years for arson, a further six months on probation, and approximately six months for falsifying documents…. Reducing the remaining thirty four months to

Wanted Poster 'Anarchist perpetrators Baader/Meinhof gang' *c.* 1971

three, nine or twelve is intended to reduce the moral justification for the 14 May breakout....

On 14 May, the cops fired the first shots. This was the case in Frankfurt as well, where two of us ran for it, because we are not going to just let ourselves be arrested. The cops shot to kill. Sometimes we don't shoot at all, and when we did, we didn't shoot to kill.... We don't 'use firearms recklessly'. The cop who finds himself in the contradiction of being a 'little man' and a capitalist pawn, a low paid employee and monopoly capitalist's agent, is not obliged to follow orders. We shoot back if someone shoots at us. The cop who lets us go, we let him go as well.

It is clear that the massive hunt for us is really directed against the entire socialist left in the Federal Republic and West Berlin. This circus cannot be justified by the small amount of money or the few cars and documents we are alleged to have stolen, or by the attempted murder they're trying to pin on us. The ruling class has been scared out of its skin. They thought that they had this state and all of its inhabitants, classes, and contradictions under control, right down to the last detail: the intellectuals reduced to their magazines, the left isolated in its own circles, Marxism–Leninism disarmed, and internationalism demoralised. However fragile it may pretend to be, the power structure is not so easily damaged. One should not be tricked by this hue and cry into contributing to all this noise.

We are not saying that the organisation of armed resistance groups can replace the legal proletarian organisations, that isolated actions can replace the class struggle, or that armed struggle can replace political work in the factories and neighbourhoods. We are arguing that armed struggle is a necessary precondition for the latter to succeed and progress, that armed struggle is 'the highest form of Marxism-Leninism', and that it can and must begin now, as without it there can be no anti-imperialist struggle in the metropole. We are not Blanquists nor are we anarchists, though we think Blanqui was a great revolutionary and the personal heroism of many anarchists is certainly above reproach.... The RAF's urban guerrilla concept is not based on an optimistic evaluation of the situation in the Federal Republic and West Berlin.... The concept of the urban guerrilla comes from Latin America. There, like here, it is the method of revolutionary intervention by generally weak revolutionary forces.

The urban guerrilla struggle is based on an understanding that there will be no Prussian-style marching orders, which so many so-called revolutionaries are waiting for to lead the people into revolutionary struggle. It is based on the analysis that by the time the conditions are right for armed struggle, it will be too late to prepare for it. It is based on the recognition that without revolutionary initiatives in a country with so much potential for violence as the Federal Republic, there will be no revolutionary orientation when the conditions for revolutionary struggle are more favourable, as they soon will be given the political and economic developments of late capitalism.

The urban guerrilla is the consequence of the long since complete negation of parliamentary democracy by the elected representatives themselves. It is the inevitable response to the Emergency Laws and the Hand Grenade Law. It is the willingness to struggle with the very means that the system appropriates for itself to neutralise its enemies. The urban guerrilla is based on facing facts, not making excuses for them....

The urban guerrilla struggle is armed struggle in a situation in which the police use their weapons recklessly and in which class justice finds Kurras not guilty and buries comrades alive. The urban guerrilla struggle means not being demoralised by the violence of the system.

The urban guerrilla aims to destroy certain aspects of the state structure, and to destroy the myth of state omnipotence and invulnerability.

The urban guerrilla requires the organisation of an illegal structure, including safe houses, weapons, cars, and documents. What one needs to know about this, Marighella describes in his *Minimanual of the Urban Guerrilla*. What needs to be known beyond that, we are always ready to tell anyone who wants to participate in the guerrilla struggle. We don't know that much yet, but we know a little bit...

The urban guerrillas struggle requires that one be totally clear about one's motivations that one not be put off by the attacks from *Bild Zeitung*, the anti-Semitic-criminal-subhuman-murderer-arsonist label that they apply to all revolutionaries. All the shit they spit out and are willing to say, and which still influences what many comrades think about us, must have no effect....

Long-term, meticulous work is crucial for the urban guerrilla, insofar as we want to go beyond discussion to action. If the option of retreating to a bourgeois profession is not kept open, if the option of leaving behind the revolution for a townhouse is not maintained, if none of this is even desirable, then, with the full pathos of Blanqui's statement, 'The duty of the revolutionary is to always struggle, in spite of everything to struggle, to struggle until death'. There is no revolutionary struggle, and there has been no revolutionary struggle, in which this hasn't shown itself to be true: Russia, China, Cuba, Algeria, Palestine, Vietnam.

Some say that the political possibilities of organisation, agitation, and propaganda are far from being exhausted, and only when they have been exhausted should one consider armed struggle. We say that the political possibilities will not be fully utilised until armed struggle is recognised as the political goal, as long as the strategic conclusion that all reactionaries are paper tigers is not grasped despite the tactical conclusion that they are criminals, murderers, and exploiters.

We will not talk about 'armed propaganda': we will do it. The prison breakout didn't take place for reasons of propaganda, but to get the guy out. The bank robberies that they try to lay at our doorstep, we'd only do that to grab the money. The 'spectacular successes' that Mao tells us we must have scored if 'the enemy paints us as utterly black' are not our successes alone. The big clamour that has been made about us is due more to the Latin American comrades—given the clear line they have already drawn between themselves and the enemy—which has led the ruling class here, suspecting us of some bank robberies, to 'energetically oppose' us, because of what we have begun to build here: the urban guerrilla in the form of the Red Army Faction....

The concentration of violent power in the hands of the few can occur unopposed if it is done quietly, if unnecessary provocation, which can set a process of solidarity in motion, is avoided—that is something that was learned as a result of the student movement and the Paris May. Therefore, the Red Cells are not yet banned. Therefore the KP can exist as the DKP without the ban on the KP being lifted. Therefore there are still some liberal television programs. And, therefore, some organisations can get away with thinking that they are not as stupid as they really are.

The comrades who only deal with the question of legality and illegality superficially have obviously misunderstood the amnesty with which the student movement was to be tamed. In lifting the criminalisation of hundreds of students, they sent them away with just a fright, preventing further radicalisation and impressing upon them the value of the privileges that come with being a bourgeois student—that in spite of the nature of the knowledge-factory, the universities are helpful to social climbers. This deepens the class divide between students and the proletariat, between their privileged everyday life and the everyday life of those who do the shit work and who were not offered the same amnesty by the same class enemy. So once again the division between theory and practice is maintained. The equation: amnesty equals pacification....

We don't count on terror and fascism provoking a spontaneous antifascist mobilisation, nor do we think that legality is always corrupt. We understand that our work offers pretexts, just as alcohol does for Willy Weyer, just as the increase in crime does for Strauß, just as *Ostpolitik* does for Barzel, just as a Yugoslav running a red light does for a taxi driver, just as a tool in the pocket does for the murderers of car thieves in Berlin. Regarding other pretexts that result from the fact that we are communists, whether communists organise and struggle will depend on whether terror and repression produce only fear and

> resignation, or whether they produce resistance, class hatred, and solidarity, and whether or not everything goes smoothly for imperialism. It depends on whether communists are so stupid as to tolerate everything that is done to them, or whether they will use legality, as well as other methods, to organise illegality, instead of fetishising one over the other....
>
> The Red Army Faction organises illegality as an offensive position for revolutionary intervention.
>
> Building the urban guerrilla means conducting the anti-imperialist struggle offensively. The Red Army Faction creates the connection between legal and illegal struggle and international struggle, between political struggle and armed struggle, and between the strategic and tactical aspects of the international communist movement. The urban guerrilla means intervening in a revolutionary way here, in spite of the weakness of the revolutionary forces in the Federal Republic and West Berlin!
>
> Cleaver said, 'Either you're part of the problem or you're part of the solution. There is nothing in between. This shit has been examined and analysed for decades and generations from every angle. My opinion is that most of what happens in this country does not need to be analysed any further'.
>
> SUPPORT THE ARMED STRUGGLE!
> VICTORY TO THE PEOPLE'S WAR!

The Federal authorities were determined to stop the so-called people's war in its tracks. In July, more than 3,000 police personnel took part in Operation Cora, the state's first serious attempt to eliminate the RAF. The operation led to the RAF suffering its first fatality. A line had had been crossed, one which would ultimately lead to an escalation of RAF violence.

On 15 July 1971, RAF members Petra Schelm and Werner Hoppe were signalled to halt at a police roadblock on Hamburg's Stressmanstraße. Instead of braking, Schelm stepped on the accelerator. A police chase ensued in which a second car and a helicopter were deployed. Eventually, the so-called 'Baader–Meinhof–Wagen' was brought to a halt. In the subsequent firefight, Schelm was killed by a bullet which struck her just below her left eye. Schelm, who was only nineteen at the time, graduated to the RAF from the hippy commune scene and the militant, anti-capitalist Roaming Hash Rebels. In particular, it was the Hash Rebel's 1969 leaflet, 'It is time to destroy', which helped to transform Schelm from a peaceful hippy into a nascent terrorist. The leaflet read:

> The Hash Rebels are the militant kernel of Berlin's counterculture. They fight against the modern monopoly capitalist system of slavery. They are fighting for their own free decisions over their bodies and form of

> life. JOIN THIS STRUGGLE. Build militant cadres in towns and cities. Contact similar groups. Shit on the society of middle age and taboos. Become wild and do beautiful things. Have a joint. Whatever you see that you don't like, destroy. Dare to struggle, dare to win.

While Schelm was certainly no innocent, there was widespread outrage at the killing of someone so young. Her boyfriend Manfred Grashof wanted to take revenge against the police, and even concocted a plan to set fire to a car outside the station where his girlfriend's killer was stationed. Then, when the police came out to investigate, he would open fire with an automatic weapon. Baader himself quashed the plan by saying that, 'We fight against imperialism, not against the cops'. In a statement released by the RAF, the shooting of Schelm was compared to that of Ohnesorg and Dutschke. The statement also promised that her death would be avenged. Over the coming months, more deaths would follow as the spiral of violence intensified.

On the night of 22/23 October, Hamburg policeman Norbert Schmid was shot and killed while trying to detain RAF members Irmgard Möller, Gerhard Möller, and Margrit Schiller. Meanwhile, Meinhof's foster mother Renate Riemech (a noted historian and peace activist) reacted against the RAF's violence by penning a letter to *Konkret* which was published the following month. The letter stated that, 'The Federal Republic is not the place for an urban guerrilla movement in the Latin American style. The country offers, at most, suitable conditions for a gangster drama'. Unsurprisingly, the letter went unanswered.

While the older generation were repelled by the RAF's violence, many of the younger generation, particularly students were increasingly identifying with the group's anti-capitalist and anti-imperialist stance. Many students carried photographs of RAF members in their wallets. Some took their hero worship to the next level by joining the group, while others 'did their bit' by offering shelter as police searches intensified. Baader came close to being captured during this deadly game of cat and mouse. Following his narrow escape, he penned a letter to the non-Springer press to prove that he was still alive, and still at large. The letter which bore Baader's thumbprint read:

> The truth of the matter is that no further information has come out about the group since the first twenty were trained in Jordan. The RAF's work is clandestine. The 'security forces', the security agencies, the police, the BND, the *Verfassungsschutz*, the BAW, *Spiegel*, and the Springer Press know nothing.
>
> They know nothing about the size, the number of members, the organisation, the firepower, or the tactics of the group. Everything

> written about us by the police state for public consumption over the past year-and-a-half is false, is speculation, or is counterpropaganda with the objective of discrediting the theory and practice of the urban guerrilla and driving a wedge between us and our base.
>
> I haven't considered turning myself in. No RAF members have considered turning themselves in. So far no RAF prisoner has provided testimony. Announcements of successes against us have only been about arrests or killings. The guerrilla's strength lies in the determination of each of us. We are not on the run. We are here organising armed resistance against the regime of the propertied classes and the ongoing exploitation of the people.
>
> The RAF's current activities are directed towards the formation of politico-military cadre, acquiring better arms and training for revolutionaries, and the anchoring of the group in a sympathetic scene that is ready to support armed resistance. The tactical line that we are currently following is to develop the propaganda of the urban guerrilla through the revolutionary organisations that are still legal and to develop broad based logistical support amongst all layers of the population.
>
> None of us see any subjective or objective basis for betraying the struggle to which we have committed ourselves; nor Genscher's dirty amnesty deal, not Ruhland, the Social Democrats' van der Lubbe, not the extensive militarisation of the police, not prison, not torture, and not the police terror against the population. 'The stones they have thrown will fall at their own feet'.
>
> If the price for our lives or our freedom is to be the betrayal of the capitalist struggle, there is only one response: we won't pay it.
>
> The armed struggle does not develop from one headline to the next. The politico-military strategy of the urban guerrilla is based on the resistance to parliamentary democracy's fascist drift and the organisation of the first regular units of the Red Army in the people's war. The battle has just begun.

However, during the first few months of 1972, it must have appeared to Baader that the battle was not in fact beginning, but instead, as the police dragnet closed in, it was all but lost.

On 2 March, the police raided a Hamburg apartment used by the RAF to produce forged documents. Despite fearing that the location had already been compromised, Manfred Grashof, the RAF's specialist in forged paperwork decided to go there with his accomplice Wolfgang Grundmann to pick up some valuable items. On arrival, they were surprised by three policemen. While Grundmann opted for immediate surrender, Grashof decided to fight it out. Thinking that the police were operating a shoot to kill policy, he fired first, hitting Police Chief Superintendent Hans Eckhardt in the chest and stomach with two illegal dum-dum bullets. Eckhardt later died from the massive injuries to his internal organs. Grashof was himself then shot in the chest and head. Despite his injuries, he was later moved from the hospital to a regular prison cell on the orders of Federal Supreme Court Judge Wolfgang Buddenberg.

Also on 2 March, the police closed in on a young couple in Augsberg who had been under surveillance for several weeks. Thomas Weissbecher, a former member of the Roaming Hash Rebels who had recently graduated to the RAF was shot and killed by a policeman with an itchy trigger finger. His partner, Carmen Roll, a former member of the Socialist Patients' Collective was taken in to custody, whereafter she was given large doses of narcotics during a chemically induced interrogation which almost led to her death. The harsh treatment of Grashof and Roll characterised the new hard-line approach to terrorism by the Federal authorities.

In early 1972, the Free University in Berlin appointed the Internationalist and Marxist Ernest Mandel as their professor of economics. Swiftly, the Berlin Senate moved in to veto the appointment. Meanwhile, amnesties were being offered to those rebellious students and youths who wished to renounce the class struggle and re-join the establishment. The RAF response to the hard-line stance adopted by the police and judiciary, the purging of the universities, and the state's attempt to bribe the nation's youth came in two forms: the release of their most comprehensive statement to date, and a coordinated bombing campaign. The theoretical document released by the RAF in April 1972 was almost twice as long as its predecessor. While on the surface the document appears as a characteristic example of RAF theoretical onanism, it nonetheless contains what appears to be a genuine attempt to find strategic connections between the struggles of the working class and the guerrilla movement. In a section entitled *The Militarisation of the Class Struggle*, these strategic connections become apparent:

> In spite of capital's strength and the weakness of the working class, the state is arming itself and preparing for the militarisation of the class struggle. The political means correspond with the economic facts: capital's aggression. The political facts signal the extent and the strength of the attack.
>
> The less the common good—which is to say general affluence, increasing income, and improved living conditions for all—is addressed by capitalist policy, the more it must be promoted, so as to reduce possibilities for criticising the methods employed by capital. Therefore, critical journalists have been fired everywhere; therefore the schools have been cleared of leftists; therefore, the CSU has seized control of the

> *Bayerischen Rundfunk*, which can only signal the acquisition of ARD stations by the ZDF—even if the process can't proceed as quickly in other Länder.
>
> To the extent that the system can no longer purchase the loyalty of the masses, they must be coerced. As it will no longer be given willingly, it will be gained through threats and violence; the BGS will be transformed into a federal police force and increased from a force of 23,000 to 30,000; the police will be armed with submachine guns, and the citizenry should become accustomed to seeing submachine gun-armed police on street corners as they are of paying taxes; penal law will be stiffened; emergency exercises will be conducted using sharpshooters; comrades will be taken into preventative custody; RAF suspects will be subject to the death penalty.
>
> To the extent that people have no further reason, once capitalism is finally enforced in West Germany, to continue being anti-communist, communists must be forcibly separated from the people. Therefore, the left is being pushed out of the factories.... Capitalist propagandists use the narrow opportunity that the Red Army affords them to argue that their core problem, the escalation of the class struggle, is caused by us, and that the rise of right-wing radicalism is a response to us. This is objectively the argument of the class enemy and subjectively an entirely shallow approach based on nothing more than the superficial assessment of the issues found in the bourgeois press.

The importance of this, *Serve the People: The Urban Guerrilla and Class Struggle,* lies not so much in its content, but in the fact that it was the last theoretical document to be released by the RAF from outside the confines of a prison cell for almost ten years. It also presaged the RAF's 'May Offensive' which coincided with America's escalation of the war in Vietnam.

The RAF offensive began on 11 May with the bombing of an American military base and the site of the National Security Agency in Frankfurt-am-Main. Colonel Paul A. Bloomquist was killed, and thirteen other personnel were injured in the blasts. A press statement issued a few days later by the RAF demanded an end to the bombing of Hanoi and Haiphong, and the immediate withdrawal of American troops from Vietnam. The following day, bombs were set off in the Police headquarters in Augsberg and in the car park of the Land Office of Criminal Investigations in Munich. Both blasts caused considerable damage, though fortunately, no one was killed.

On 16 May, a car bomb destroyed Federal Judge Wolfgang Buddenberg's car. Buddenberg was not in the car at the time, but his wife Gerta, who was on her way to pick him up from work in the car, was seriously injured. Three days later, a team led by Meinhof detonated bombs in the proof-readers' room and the toilets of the Springer Press building in Hamburg. The blasts injured seventeen employees, two seriously. This particular bombing proved to be a propaganda own-goal for the RAF as some sections of the left were unhappy about workers being targeted. On 24 May, two cars loaded with explosives detonated near a data processing centre and the officer's club at the American military headquarters at Heidelberg. Three soldiers were killed, and six injured in the blasts designed to 'commemorate' the anniversary of the death of RAF member Petra Schlem.

Towards the end of the month, the police launched a major operation to capture the entire leadership of the RAF. On 1 June, Baader, and two other RAF members were cornered as they arrived at a compromised safe house in Frankfurt-am-Main. Baader was shot in the leg by a police sniper following a tense standoff involving three hundred police personnel and an armoured car. A week later, Gudrun Ensslin was arrested in a shop in Hamburg's fashionable Jungfernstieg Boulevard. On 15 June, Meinhof and her accomplice Gerhard Möller were arrested in Hannover after being turned in to the police by a left-wing trade unionist who had agreed to put them up for the night. The arrests went on until early July, by which time the entire leadership of the RAF were behind bars. Those few surviving members still at large concentrated on dodging the authorities. Meanwhile, from their prison cells, the RAF leadership continued the struggle by expressing their solidarity with the Palestinian Black September group and by starting a series of hunger strikes.

In November 1972, the RAF issued their first statement from behind bars. The statement entitled *Black September Action in Munich: Regarding the Strategy for the Anti-Imperialist Struggle* focused on the geopolitics of anti-imperialism, critics of the armed struggle, and solidarity with the Palestinian guerrillas who had carried out the Munich massacre. These extracts from the statement demonstrate the extent of the RAF's sympathetic attitude towards the Black September group:

> The Black September action in Munich has simultaneously clarified both the nature of the imperialist ruling class and the anti-imperialist struggle, in a way that no revolutionary action in West Germany or West Berlin has. It was simultaneously anti-imperialist, anti-fascist, and internationalist. It indicated an understanding of historical and political connections, that are always the province of the people—that is to say, those from whom the profit is sucked, those who are free from complicity with the system, those who have no reason to believe the illusions fostered by their oppressors, no reason to accept the fantasy their oppressors pass off as history, no reason to pay the slightest attention to their version of reality. It revealed the rage and the strength that these revolutionaries

get from their close connection to the Palestinian people, a connection resulting in a class consciousness that makes their historical mission to act as a vanguard perfectly clear....

BLACK SEPTEMBER'S STRATEGY IS THE REVOLUTIONARY STRATEGY FOR ANTI-IMPERIALIST STRUGGLE, BOTH IN THE THIRD WORLD AND IN THE METROPOLE, GIVEN THE IMPERIALIST CONDITIONS CREATED BY MULTINATIONAL CORPORATIONS.

The comrades from Black September who had their own Black September in 1970 when the Jordanian army massacred 20,000 Palestinians, went back to the place that is the origin of the massacre: West Germany—formerly Nazi Germany—now at the centre of imperialism. Back to the site of the power that forced the Jews of both West and East Europe to immigrate to Israel. Back to those who had hoped to profit from the theft of Palestinian land. Back to where Israel got its reparation payments and, until 1965, officially, its weapons. Back to where the Springer Corporation celebrated Israel's 1967 Blitzkrieg in an anti-Communist orgy. Back to the supplier who provided Hussein's army with panzers, assault rifles, machine-pistols, and munitions. Back to where everything possible was done—using diplomatic aid, oil deals, investments, weapons, and diplomatic relationships—to pit Arab regimes against each other, and to turn all of them against the Palestinian movement. Back to the place from which imperialism launches its bombers when other means of repressing the Arab liberation movement fail: West Germany—Munich—the NATO airport at Fürstenfeldbruck....

Black September has brought its war from the Arab periphery of imperialism into the centre.... The centre is the U.S.A., Japan, and West Europe under the leadership of the FRG.... Their weapons production is only one of the sectors of their productive capacity that is directed against the liberation movements, their price controls for raw materials constitute just one of the many ways they ensure their rule over the Third World.... Their weapons consist of the potential of capital, technology, the means of communication and information control, and the means of transportation. Their strategy for conquest is based on investments, transfer of profits, information policy, diversification, marketing, sales planning, and stockpiling. Their occupier or colonial ideology means controlling currency and creating work. Their goal is to assimilate, repress, and rob—the alternative offered is starvation and extermination....

The bomb attack on the Strüver Corporation in Hamburg was an attack on one of Israel's military suppliers. With their action at the Olympic

Village, they brought the conflict between the imperialist metropole of Israel and the Palestinians from the periphery of the system into its centre—they tore off the FRG's 'constitutional' mask and revealed the true objective nature of imperialism's façade: that they are waging war against the liberation movements of the Third World and that their final objective is strategic extermination and fascism.... The Black September action in Munich leaves no room for misunderstanding. They took hostages from a people who are carrying out an extermination policy against them. They put their lives on the line to free their comrades. They didn't want to die. They put off their ultimatum. In the face of the uncompromising attitude advocated by Israel, they held the Israeli hostages prisoner. The Israeli hostages understood that this was a last resort. They were betrayed by the German authorities just as the revolutionaries were. The German police massacred the hostages and the revolutionaries.

The Black September action in Munich will live on in the memory of the anti-imperialist struggle. The death of the Arab comrades weighs as heavily as Mount Tai.

THE STONES THAT THESE BEASTS THREW AT FÜRSTENFELDBRUCK WILL FALL AT THEIR OWN FEET!
SOLIDARITY WITH THE LIBERATION STRUGGLE OF THE PALESTINIAN PEOPLE!
SOLIDARITY WITH THE VIETNAMESE REVOLUTION!
REVOLUTIONARIES OF ALL COUNTRIES UNITE!

Meinhof added to the group's already manifestly repugnant anti-Semitic tone when she was asked to comment on the Munich massacre during RAF member Horst Mahler's trial. Without hesitation, she stated that, 'Finance capital and the banks, the hard core of the system of imperialism and capitalism had turned the hatred of men against money and exploitation, and against the Jews.... Auschwitz.... meant that six million Jews were killed and then thrown on the waste-heap of Europe for what they were considered: money Jews'. There is no doubt that such vile comments served to further diminish support for the RAF. Richard Huffman, the noted historian of the group, noted in an interview about the perceptions of radical women that Meinhof and the RAF 'became fantastically anti-Israel and pro-Palestine'. He went on to add that, 'They defined their stance as anti-Zionism, but most people didn't buy it, including me'. The blatant anti-Semitism of the RAF was one of the factors which eventually led to the group's political isolation.

While what was left of the RAF attempted to regroup, the incarcerated leadership were separated from each other by being held in prisons around

RAF pamphlet supporting the actions of the Palestinian Black September group.

the country. Baader was held in the Schwalmstadt (Düsseldorf), while Ensslin was held in Essen, Meinhof in Cologne, Meins in Wittlich (Cologne), Möller in Rastatt (Baden), Müller in Hamburg, Raspe in Cologne, and Mahler in Moabit (Berlin). All the prisoners were kept in solitary confinement and were subjected to sensory deprivation. The use of such methods had been pioneered by Dr Jan Gross of the Eppendorf University Hospital (Hamburg) in the late 1950s. Gross found that prolonged periods of sensory deprivation induced problems with concentration, sleeplessness, and panic attacks. The use of sensory deprivation characterised 'a new ruthlessness in dealing with terrorists that was often at odds with the self-proclaimed objective of defending democracy'. Astrid Proll later described her experiences in Ossendorf Prison's 'Dead Wing':

> ... I was taken to an empty wing, a dead wing, where I was the only prisoner. Ulrike Meinhof later called it the 'Silent Wing'. The shocking experience was that I could not hear any noises apart from the ones I generated myself. Nothing. Absolute silence. I went through stages of excitement, I was haunted by visual and acoustic hallucinations. There were extreme disturbances of concentration and attacks of weakness. I had no idea how long this would go on for. I was terrified that I would go

> mad. During the two-and-a-half years on remand I was four-and-a-half months completely isolated in the Dead Wing of Cologne–Ossendorf. Not even today, six years later, have I completely recovered from that. I can't stand rooms which are painted white because they remind me of my cell. Silence in a wood can terrify me; it reminds me of the silence in the isolated cell. Darkness makes me so depressive as if my life were taken away. Solitude causes me as much fear as crowds. Even today I have the feeling occasionally as if I can't move.

Following her arrest, Meinhof was held in similar conditions. After 237 days of this 'dehumanisation through social isolation', she wrote about how she survived this special brand of torture:

> I finally realised I had to pull myself out of this, I myself had no right to let these frightful things keep affecting me—it was my duty to fight my way out of it. By whatever means there are of doing that in prison: daubing the walls, coming to blows with a cop, wrecking the fitments, hunger strike. I wanted to make them at least put me under arrest, because then you got to hear something—you don't have a radio babbling away, only the bible to read, maybe no mattress, no windows, etc.—but that's a different kind of torture from not hearing anything. And obviously it would have been a relief to me....

In addition to their isolation within the prison environment, the RAF prisoners were largely cut off from the outside world. Prison visits were limited to lawyers and family members. All visits by family members were supervised and their conversations recorded for possible use in evidence at the forthcoming trials process.

On 27 August 1974, Meinhof was transferred to Berlin in order to stand trial for her part in the freeing of Baader four years earlier. Then, on 29 November, she was sentenced to eight years' imprisonment. During the course of the trial, forty members of the RAF started a second hunger strike intended to draw the world's attention to their harsh treatment behind bars. Not surprisingly, the authorities paid little heed to the hunger strikers' demands. On 2 February 1975, the RAF at large published a statement in which they exhorted their comrades to discontinue their hunger strike:

> To the RAF prisoners:
> We are asking you to call off your hunger strike now even though the demand for an end to isolation has not yet been met. This demand has not been met because of the powerful reactionary mobilisation and the class offensive from above, the subjective conditions of an underdeveloped

class struggle, the corruption of the proletariat's class organisations, and the weakness of the revolutionary left.

Understand that this is an order.

The fact is that the legal left, as a result of their defensiveness and helplessness in the face of the new fascism, has not developed the capacity to organise solidarity as a weapon, and has failed to develop in a way that corresponds to the construction of the guerrilla and the politics of the RAF.

The strike has brought them face-to-face with reality: the weakness of political strategies that ignore the need to establish and develop the capacity to act from the underground, the necessity for armed politics as the concrete expression of proletarian internationalism here. Our massive mobilisation in 68 was followed by a series of setbacks: the splits, the sects, and the corruption that forced us onto the defensive.

We are saying that the prisoners' strike has done everything it could to mediate, mobilise, and organise anti-imperialist politics here. Its escalation would not contribute anything qualitative to the struggle.

The state has calculated that it will be able to create propaganda from the execution of guerrilla prisoners—who struggle, always struggle, in spite of everything struggle—that would make resistance seem hopeless. Allowing you to continue in this situation would amount to sacrificing you.

We are taking this weapon away from you, because the prisoners' struggle—given the existing balance of power—is now something that we must settle with our weapons.

VICTORY WILL BE OURS!

While the authorities began the process of prosecuting the RAF leadership for murder, attempted murder, and the formation of a criminal association, the radical left took the initiative by launching a series of guerrilla actions.

On 27 February, the 2 June Movement kidnapped the Berlin Christian Democrat leader and mayoral candidate Peter Lorenz. Lorenz was released on 5 March following the intervention of Heinrich Albertz whom the group had asked to act as an intermediary. Then, on 24 April, the RAF took eleven hostages at the German Embassy in Stockholm in an attempt to coerce the authorities into releasing the group's leadership from prison. The plan went disastrously wrong when after executing two hostages, one of the group accidentally set off explosive charges which destroyed most of the building. In the explosion, RAF member Ulrich Wessel was killed and five others injured. The German Ambassador, Dieter Stoecker was also wounded. This act of terrorism was followed on 23 September by the detonation of a large bomb at Hamburg's main railway station which injured eleven people. The year of carnage was crowned by the 'Arm of the Arab Revolution' attack on the Organisation of the Petroleum Exporting Countries (OPEC) headquarters on 21 December. The attack, led by Carlos the Jackal resulted in the murder of an Austrian policemen, an Iraqi OPEC official, and a Libyan economist. Ten OPEC officials, along with twenty-five others were held until the guerrillas were flown to Algiers the following day.

Meanwhile, the trial of the RAF leadership had got underway at the specially built courtroom within the Stammheim Prison complex. As the trial dragged on interminably, Meinhof found herself increasingly isolated within the group. On 4 May 1976, while filing her demands for the production of evidence, Ensslin had distanced herself and the group from the 1972 bombing of the Springer Press building in Hamburg. Five days after this first discernible split in the RAF leadership, Meinhof was found dead in her prison cell. The mysterious circumstances of her death produced a storm of protest from all sections of the leftist scene. An open letter signed by leftist luminaries Jean-Paul Sartre and Simone de Beauvoir equated Meinhof's death with the worst excesses of the Nazi era.

On 15 May, approximately 7,000 people attended Meinhof's funeral in West Berlin. Many had their faces blackened to avoid identification by the police. Following the funeral, many of the mourners joined demonstrations in central Berlin and at the Moabit courthouse. Three days later, demonstrators clashed with the police in West Berlin. On 2 June, the American Army Headquarters and Officer's Club in Frankfurt-am-Main were bombed by the 'Ulrike Meinhof Commando'. The international terrorist community were also quick to respond. On 27 June, two members of the Popular Front for the Liberation of Palestine and two members of German revolutionary cells hijacked an Air France flight carrying 248 passengers from Tel Aviv to Paris. The aircraft was flown to Entebbe in Uganda where the non-Jewish passengers were released. The guerrilla's demands that fifty-three prisoners (including six members of the RAF) be released were refused by the authorities who had taken an even sterner line in their dealings with terrorists. The impasse was not broken until 4 July, when Operation Thunderbolt was launched by elements of the Israeli Defence Forces. In the ensuing action, 102 of the remaining 106 hostages were freed. None of the hijackers survived.

On 29 March 1977, imprisoned RAF and 2 June Movement members began another hunger strike, the objective of which was to secure Prisoner of War status. Their comrades at large supported the prisoners' struggle by assassinating the attorney general Siegfried Buback on 7 April. However, his assassination failed to prevent the announcement on 28 April that Baader, Ensslin and Raspe had been sentenced to life imprisonment.

These sentences prompted active RAF members in the field to step up their terror campaign. On 30 July, three RAF guerrillas attempted to kidnap the head of the Dresdner Bank, Jürgen Ponto. The attempt was bungled, and Ponto was shot five times. He died in a pool of blood on his own kitchen floor. The RAF then went for broke on 5 September by kidnapping Martin Schleyer, the head of the employer's association of the Federal Union of German Industry. Within a day of the kidnapping, the guerrillas issued their demand for the release of eleven members of the RAF leadership. Meanwhile, Schleyer was held captive by the group, and it was not until 13 October that a photograph of him was released. With negotiations between the RAF guerrillas and the authorities deadlocked, a Palestinian group known as the Struggle Against World Imperialism Organisation acted in solidarity with their German comrades by hijacking a Lufthansa jet flying from Majorca to Frankfurt-am-Main. After landing at Mogadishu Airport in Somalia, German Special Forces stormed the aircraft. During the assault they killed three hijackers, wounded a fourth, and released all eighty-six hostages.

The following morning at 07:00 hrs the authorities publicly announced the successful outcome of the operation to release the passengers and crew. The news quickly filtered back to the RAF leadership in prison. One hour later, the prison authorities announced the suicide of Baader and Ensslin, and the attempted suicides of Raspe and Möller. In reprisal, the RAF at large executed Schleyer on 18 October, dumping his body in a car which was found the following day in the border town of Mulhouse. The violent RAF terror campaign conducted in September and October 1977 alienated many people. Furthermore, this last explosion of targeted violence failed to secure any of its objectives. In essence, the period known as the 'German Autumn' marked the end of a prolonged class and anti-imperialist struggle started by Baader and Ensslin in 1968. Later, an RAF statement acknowledged the political realities of the situation by stating that, 'We made errors in 77, and the offensive was turned into our most serious defeat'. The RAF retreated to lick their wounds and reformulate their strategy. While their campaign of violence continued throughout the 1980s and 1990s, they were increasingly regarded by the wider public as political anachronisms. Finally, realising that their time was over, the RAF officially dissolved itself in 1998.

20

Authority Gives Way to Possibility

On 5 May 1789, a great revolution began in France and its colonies which would ultimately lead to the overthrow of the monarchy, the establishment of the republic, the corruption of the Directory, and the dictatorship of Napoleon Bonaparte. This revolution challenged the long-held assumption that political power could be based upon inherited legitimacy. Two hundred years later, these same assumptions were being challenged by the peoples of Eastern Europe. The Communist regimes had based their claims to power on a political theory which was rooted in the so-called 'engine of history'. However, dialectical materialism gave no clues to the impending social explosion which shook Communism to its core. While the French Revolution was a bloody affair, the social revolutions across Eastern Europe were largely characterised by the peaceful transition from one form of government to another. This peaceful transition was only possible because the leader of the Soviet Union decided to take the brave decision of letting history take its course.

The course of history which led to the downfall of Communism, the fall of the Berlin Wall and the liberation from tyranny of the people of Eastern Europe is not clearly defined. However, we may conclude that the process was a protracted one, which in this author's view began with the June 1953 worker's uprising in East Berlin. Other events to take into consideration must include the 1956 Hungarian uprising, the 1968 Prague Spring, the Soviet economic downturn during the 1970s, the unpopular war in Afghanistan, and the emergence of 'great actors' on the political scene such as Vaclav Havel, Mikhail Gorbachev, Margaret Thatcher, Pope John Paul II, Ronald Reagan, and Lech Wałesa. Between them, these people changed the course of history.

It was the British prime minister, Margaret Thatcher who first noticed that a new wind was blowing through the Kremlin. Following his election by the

Mikhail Gorbachev and Erich Honecker singing the 'Internationale' at the East German Communist Party's 11th Congress in April 1986.

Politburo to general secretary of the Communist Party of the Soviet Union in 1985, Gorbachev instituted reforms which effectively blew away the cobwebs clinging to the stagnant institutions which made up the monolithic state. Following a visit to London, Thatcher was asked by reporters what she thought of the new Soviet leader. 'I'm cautiously optimistic' she replied. 'I like Mr Gorbachev. We can do business together'. Within a short time she also managed to convince the American President, Ronald Reagan that this was a very different kind of Soviet leader. At their subsequent meeting in Geneva, Reagan and Gorbachev established a rapport. In December 1987, Gorbachev's first visit to America ushered in a period of 'Gorbymania' during which *Time* magazine named him 'Man of the Year'.

Meanwhile in East Berlin, the long-serving party leader Erich Honecker was taking his inspiration not from the reformer Gorbachev, but from the Chinese leader Deng Xiaoping, whose brutal suppression of dissent in Beijing's Tiananmen Square resonated with the ageing despot. Honecker's long-serving Stasi chief Erich Mielke warned that 'hostile opposing forces and groups have already achieved a measure of power and are using all methods to achieve a change in the balance of power'. For the brutal Mielke, the application of force was the only answer. Former Stasi Colonel Rainer Wiegand was present when he praised Deng's response to the

Ronald Reagan and Mikhail Gorbachev on friendly terms *c.* 1988.

protests at Tiananmen Square. According to Wiegand, 'Mielke said our situation was comparable and we had to be ready to counter it with all means and methods'. The Chinese leadership had succeeded in smothering the protests before the situation got out of hand. However, neither Honecker nor Mielke completely understood what was really happening as their Marxist–Leninist analytical tools were simply not up to the job.

During early September 1989, thousands of East Germans holidaying in Hungary took advantage of the government's decision to dismantle the barbed wire fortifications along the Austrian border. Instead of heading home to their dreary East German apartments, they elected to travel to Austria. Soon, thousands more were making the journey to Hungary via Czechoslovakia. In Prague, the roads filled with abandoned Trabant cars provided tangible proof of the extent of the exodus. Honecker and Mielke responded by persuading the Czechoslovakian government to close its border to East Germans. While this move staunched the flow of refugees, it created at the same time a political crisis as thousands of East Germans found themselves trapped in Prague. Following negotiations with the Czechoslovakian and West German governments, Honecker announced on 29 September that he would permit the refugees to leave for West Germany on board a special train. For the increasingly out of touch leader, this was simply an exercise in ridding his regime of 'antisocial elements who trample on moral values'. However, when news of the special train became known, thousands more demanded the right to leave. People sensed that this was their moment, and they were no longer afraid. From this moment on, the crisis developed a momentum of its own.

On 7 October, the deeply unpopular East German regime celebrated its fortieth anniversary with a parade of Stalin-esque proportions. Gorbachev felt somewhat ill at ease attending these celebrations for a regime that had become an anachronism. Thousands of protestors gathered outside the State Council building demanding their freedom, and shouting 'Gorby, Gorby, Gorby, help us'. Gorbachev had confided to his aides that he was 'disgusted by Honecker's inept handling of the crisis'. Now at the moment of decision, he advised Honecker to adopt Soviet style economic and political reforms before it was too late. In an impromptu speech before East German party leaders, Gorbachev emphasised the urgency of the situation by stating pointedly that, 'Life will punish those who arrive too late'. Reflecting on the East German leader's obstinacy, he later recalled that, 'Comrade Honecker obviously considers himself No.1 in socialism, if not in the world. He did not really perceive any more what was actually going on'. For Gorbachev, Honecker was a lost cause.

Following his return to Moscow, the Soviet leader ordered the general staff to ensure that Soviet troops in East Germany remained in their

Abandoned Trabants symbolising the collapse of a bankrupt political system. (*Wikimedia Commons*)

barracks. Honecker was unwilling to listen to reason, and therefore Gorbachev had no other alternative than to abandon him. 'What will be will be, let history take its course' said the pragmatic Soviet leader. Indeed, history was taking its course, and for Honecker's regime, that meant that the end was not far off.

The day after Gorbachev left for Moscow, between 70,000 and 200,000 protesters marched through the streets of Leipzig, many of whom carried placards demanding the right to free elections. Honecker ordered the police to use any means to disperse the protesters. However, the local police commanders did not want to have a Tiananmen Square massacre on their hands and so ignored the orders from Berlin. The events in Leipzig destroyed what was left of Honecker's authority. A battle within the Politburo ensued. The ageing despot was ousted and replaced by the youngest member of the ruling body, the Chief of Internal Security, Egon Krenz. His attempts to portray himself as the East German Gorbachev failed, the new party slogan, 'Change and Renewal' failing to resonate with people who demanded radical change. For Krenz too, the prospect of change and renewal quickly vanished when he discovered from his planning chief Gerhard Schürer that the man whom he had regarded as a surrogate father and mentor had kept him in the dark about the true extent of East Germany's financial crisis. In desperation, Krenz approached the West German government for a loan, only to be told that his regime would first have to dissolve itself and allow free elections.

At the end of October 1989, large-scale demonstrations in Dresden and Leipzig broke out with protestors demanding an end to the Communist regime. On 4 November, protests in Berlin's Alexanderplatz forced Krenz into making a number of conciliatory gestures. However, this response only served to embolden the protestors into demanding more and more concessions. The border with Czechoslovakia was reopened, but even this was not enough. The embattled leader responded by firing his entire cabinet and two-thirds of the Politburo on 7 November. He also agreed to relax (not eliminate) the restrictions on travel to the West in order to relieve tensions. However, what Krenz did not anticipate, was that a subordinate would misinterpret his orders.

On the evening of 9 November, the newly appointed Communist Party spokesman Günter Schabowski read out a series of decrees, amongst them one concerning foreign travel. For the assembled press, this was a revelation. East Germans could now travel to the West. Following a ripple of excited murmuring, one reporter shouted out the question, 'When does it take effect'. A rather flustered Schabowski scratched his head, turned and muttered to his aides, then perched his spectacles on the end of his nose, before blurting out the reply, 'Immediately. Without delay'.

After being asked if the new rules also applied for travel to West Berlin, Schabowski shrugged his shoulders, shuffled some papers, and then replied, 'Permanent exit can take place via all border crossings from the GDR to West Germany and West Berlin respectively'. Asked what was going to happen to the Berlin Wall, he could only mumble incoherently before closing the press conference.

The flustered spokesman was largely oblivious to the earthquake his words had caused. After all, he had only glanced through the two-page document containing the new regulations. If he had read it more thoroughly, he would have realised that the decree was not due to come into force until the following day and that travel to the West would have been subject to the usual red tape. While Krenz had hoped that this major concession would release some steam, Schabowski's poor handling of the press conference effectively blew the boiler to pieces.

Within minutes, word filtered out that the wall was open. It was not, but that did not stop thousands of people descending on the crossing points. At the Bornholmer Straße crossing point, Major Harald Jäger, the deputy chief of the Passport Control Unit was feeling particularly anxious. With only sixty men to hold back a crowd of thousands he simply did not know

Günter Schabowski's shambolic press conference sparked the fall of the Berlin Wall.

what to do. With no orders forthcoming other than that he should try and placate the demonstrators, he took matters into his own hands in order to prevent the destruction of property and the loss of life. Shortly after 23:00 hrs he gave the order for the steel gates to be opened. A few wary individuals walked through. The trickle then became a flood as thousands walked on towards their first taste of freedom in the West. Families were reunited, and complete strangers hugged each other. As a result of this incredibly powerful expression of people power, the dreaded Berlin Wall had finally been breached.

As authority gave way to possibility, the Communist state imploded as pictures of people attacking the wall with sledgehammers and chisels were beamed live on television around the world. On 6 December 1989, Krenz resigned and was replaced as premier by Communist reformer Hans Modrow. The day before, the attorney general had instituted legal proceedings against Stasi chief Erich Mielke on charges of corruption. The eighty-two-year-old was arrested and placed in solitary confinement pending trial. With Mielke in prison, the process of disbanding the Stasi began.

On 15 January 1990, a crowd of people accelerated the process by demanding entry to the fortress-like Stasi headquarters. Outnumbered, and unsure how to react, the small detachment of police on duty opened the gates to avoid a violent confrontation. Later that evening, the new party leader arrived on the scene, only to be met with calls of 'Red Pig', and 'Down with the Communist Party'. For Modrow, the game was up. Two months later he was voted out of office in the first genuinely free election in that part of Germany since 1932.

Meanwhile, Mielke went on trial, during the course of which he appeared to be increasingly confused and decrepit. While on remand he was given a red telephone which was similar to the ones in his Stasi headquarters. Although the telephone was not connected, it appears that the rapidly ageing former Stasi chief enjoyed making imaginary calls to his agents. This behaviour, whether contrived or not, served as an indicator of his failing mental health. In 1995, parole officers and lawyers successfully argued that he was 'totally confused'. All charges against him were subsequently dropped, and after spending 1,904 days in detention, he was freed to live in a small, two-roomed flat. Mielke died in a Berlin nursing home aged 92 on 21 May 2000. His office in the former Stasi headquarters in Berlin is now a popular museum exhibit for adherents of Ostalgie (a fetish and nostalgia for all aspects of East Germany).

History did not end with the fall of the Berlin Wall, but history was made. The dissolution of the Soviet Union came only two years after this momentous event. The fall of Communism ushered in a new era in

The newly opened border crossing at Potsdamer Platz *c.* 1989. (*Wikimedia Commons*)

The fall of the Berlin Wall. (*Wikimedia Commons*)

People walking through a newly-opened section of the Berlin Wall. (*Wikimedia Commons*)

Authority gives way to possibility.

A night of celebration like no other following the fall of the wall.

which the peoples of Eastern Europe regained their basic freedoms after long years of occupation. The events of 1989–1991 brought an end to the bipolar Cold War world. However, thirty years later, old geopolitical rivalries have resurfaced. Moreover, repressive, nationalistic, capitalist regimes have emerged in some former Communist states. As such, it can be argued that the great expectations resulting from that incredible night of 9 November 1989 have yet to be met.

21
Steglitz–Zehlendorf Viewpoints

Viewpoint (F1): The Allied Museum (Clayallee, 135, Berlin)

Since its inauguration in June 1998 (on the fiftieth anniversary of the Berlin airlift) the Allied Museum has documented the political and military commitments of the Western Allies in Germany, particularly West Berlin. The main themes in the museum are denazification, the Berlin airlift, and the 1961 Berlin crisis. On the museum site there are four permanent exhibitions and changing temporary exhibitions. The permanent exhibitions are: 'How enemies became friends'—main building. 'From the end of the war to the Berlin airlift'—Outpost Theatre. 'Threats to access to West Berlin'—outdoor exhibition which includes a British Hastings TG 503 aircraft, the dining car from a French military train, the last guardhouse from Check Point Charlie, and a segment of the Berlin Wall. 'From Checkpoint Charlie to the two-plus-four treaty'—Nicholson Memorial Library.

In 2008, the museum trustees expressed an interest in relocating to the former Tempelhof Airport. In 2015, the Federal authorities granted funding for the proposed move. At the time of writing (2019), the museum was still located at the Clayallee address.

The museum is free to enter and is open Tuesday–Sunday 10:00 hrs–18:00 hrs.
Tel. 0049 30 8181990
Web: www.alliiertenmuseum.de

The final incarnation of Checkpoint Charlie at the Allied Museum.

East German watchtower at the Allied Museum.

Viewpoint (F2): The Day the Wall Came Down Sculpture (Clayallee, 135, Berlin)

The monumental 'The day the wall came down' sculpture by Veryl Goodnight is located to the left of the entrance to the Allied Museum. It was the second casting of the original (1997) sculpture which stands adjacent to the Texas A&M University. The sculpture consists of five horses (one stallion and four mares) leaping over an original section of the Berlin Wall.

By using horses as her motif, Goodnight successfully transcended ethnic, political, cultural, and religious diversity among people. The horses simply represent freedom and the victory of the human spirit. The sculpture serves to remind people that political freedom should not be taken for granted. It needs to be cherished, and if necessary, defended.

The Day the Wall Came Down sculpture.

22

Coda

In 1910, Karl Scheffler famously stated that 'Berlin is a city condemned forever to becoming and never to being'. Today, Scheffler's words ring truer than ever as the great city very much remains a work in progress. While the city centre is now a thriving, bustling scene of activity thanks to massive investment in building projects around Potsdamer Platz and the government quarter, the 'vibrant pulse' of the city is steadily moving eastward. The former grey and forbidding boroughs of East Berlin are now the epicentre of 'cool' for bohemians, creatives, and thrill-seekers.

Despite ongoing gentrification, some parts of Berlin still retain the sort of gritty appeal not seen since George Orwell's first full-length work *Down and Out in Paris and London* was published. While gentrification has produced a pervading sense of homogeneity, some arbiters of taste have clung to the idea that Berlin should always be 'unique' and 'relevant'. There may indeed be something in what they say as the city is currently experiencing something of an identity crisis. Back in 2003, the mayor described Berlin as 'poor but sexy'. Today, the city appears wealthier, but thankfully is still as alluring as ever.

During its long history, Berlin has known little peace. Yet somehow this great city has emerged from the profound traumas of its past stronger, and more vibrant than ever. Perhaps this can attributed to the lack of a template for the transformation of the city. As the strict guidelines which determined the reconstruction of Dresden and Warsaw were absent, anything was possible in Berlin. The ambitious building projects which followed the fall of Communism obliterated most of the grubby arcadia of post-wall Berlin. What remains is certainly worth seeing. Indeed, the viewpoints listed by the author represent some of the most tangible evidence of the Cold War to be found anywhere in Europe.

The transformation of the city is not yet complete, and in true Berlin style, it probably never will be. Echoes of both Nazism and the Cold War continue to cast long shadows, but gradually the remains of these eras have been incorporated into the changing fabric of the city. It would be true to say that Berlin has finally come to terms with the past.

The post-wall developments on Potsdamer Platz were pivotal to the transformation of Berlin. (*Wikimedia Commons*)

Cranes continue to dominate the Berlin skyline as the transformation of the city continues. (*Wikimedia Commons*)

Select Bibliography

Books

Arandelovic, B., *Public Art and Urban Memorials in Berlin* (Springer 2018)
Berman, I., and Waller, J. M., *Dismantling Tyranny: Transitioning Beyond Totalitarian Regimes* (Rowman & Littlefield 2006)
Cochran, T. B., Norris, R. S., and Bukharin, O. A., *Making The Bomb: From Stalin To Yeltsin*
(Westview Press 1995)
Cook, C., *The Routledge Guide to European Political Archives: Sources Since 1945* (Routledge 2012)
Dennis, M., Laporte, N., *The Stasi: Myth and Reality* (Routledge 2014)
Dirke (Von), S., *All Power to the Imagination: The West German Counterculture from the Student Movement to the Greens* (University of Nebraska Press 2018)
Dobbs, M., *Six Months in 1945: From World War to Cold War* (Alfred A. Knopf 2012)
Donovan F., *Bridge In The Sky* (David McKay Inc. 1968)
Ertle, J. E., *Walled In: A West German Girls Journey To Freedom* (Mentobe Press 2013)
Fink, C., Gassert, P., and Junker, D., (eds). *1968: The World Transformed* (Cambridge University Press 1998)
Flemming, T., *Berlin in the Cold War* (Berlinica 2009)
Gaddis, J. L., *The Cold War* (Penguin Books 2005)
Gearson, J., and Schake, K., *The Berlin Wall Crisis: Perspectives of Cold War Alliances* (Palgrave 2002)
Giangreco, D. M., and Griffin, R. E., *Airbridge to Berlin: The Berlin Crisis of 1948* (Pesidio 1988)
Holloway, D., *The Soviet Union and Atomic Energy, 1939–1956* (New Haven: Yale University Press 1994)
Hopf, T., *Reconstructing the Cold War: The Early Years, 1945–1958* (Oxford University Press 2012)
Issacs, J & Downing, T., *Cold War* (Abacus 2008)
Klimke, M., and Scharloth, J., *1968 in Europe: A History of Protest and Activism, 1956–1977* (Springer 2008)

LADD, B., *Companion Guide to Berlin* (Companion Guides 2004)

LEAHY, W. D., *I Was There* (Ayer Co Pub 1979)

LIU, X., *A Partnership for Disorder* (Cambridge University Press 1996)

LORD, C. *Proconsuls: Delegated Political-Military Leadership from Rome to America today* (Cambridge University Press)

LÖWY, M., and SAYRE, R., *Romanticism against the tide of Modernity* (Duke University Press 2002)

MAN, J., *Berlin Blockade* (Ballantine Books Inc. 1973)

MARSHALL, B., *Willy Brandt: A Political Biography* (Springer 1996)

MEE, C. L. Jr., *Meeting at Potsdam* (M. Evans & Company, Inc. 1975)

MIARD-DELACROIX, H., *Willy Brandt: Life of a Statesman* (I.B. Tauris 2016)

MILLINGTON,R,. *State, Society and Memories of the Uprising of 17 June 1953 in the GDR* (Springer 2014)

MONTEFIORE, S. S., *Stalin: The Court of the Red Tsar* (W&N 2014)

NAIMARK, N. M., McDONNELL, R., and McDONNELL, F., *The Russians in Germany: A History of the Soviet Zone of Occupation 1945-1949* (Harvard University Press 1995)

NELSON, D. J., *Wartime Origins of the Berlin Dilemma* (University of Alabama Press 1978)

PHILLIPS, M., *Escape to Freedom* (Rosetta Books 2013)

SANDLER, D., *Counterpreservation: Architectural Decay in Berlin Since 1989* (Cornell University Press 2016)

SCHEIDER, P., *Berlin Now: The Rise of the City and the Fall of the Wall* (Penguin UK 2014)

SMITH, J., and MONCOURT, A., *The Red Army Faction–A documentary History* volume 1: *Projectiles for the People* (Kerslebedep Publishing 2009)

SONNEVEND, J., *Stories Without Borders: The Berlin Wall and the Making of an Iconic Event* (Oxford University Press 2016)

STEVENS, Q., and FRANK, K. A., *Memorials as Spaces of Engagement: Design, Use and Meaning* (Routledge 2015)

TURNE, B., *The Berlin Airlift: The Relief Operation that defined the Cold War* (Icon Books 2017)

VAN DEMARK, Brian., *Pandora's Keepers: Nine Men and the Atomic Bomb* (Hachette UK 2003)

VOWINKEL, A., PAYK, M. M., and LINDENBERGER, T., *Cold War Cultures: Perspectives on Eastern and Western Societies* (Berghahn Books 2012)

WALTON, D., and SUAREZ, J. A., (eds) *Culture, Space, and Power: Blurred Lines* (Lexington Press 2015)

WÜSTENBERG, J., *Civic Society and Memory in Postwar Germany* (Cambridge University Press 2017)